S0-AAB-515

# Creating High Performance

# Software Development Teams

ISBN 0-13-085083-7

90000

9 780130 850836

# Creating High Performance Software Development Teams

Frank P. Ginac

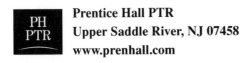

Prentice Hall PTR
Upper Saddle River, NJ 07458
www.prenhall.com

**Library of Congress Cataloging-in-Publication Data**

```
Ginac, Frank P.
  Creating high performance software development teams / by Frank P.
    Ginac
      p.  cm.
    ISBN 0-13-085083-7
    1. Comput  er software--Development--Management.I. Title
    QA76.76.D47 G555 2000
    005.1'068'4--dc21
```
                                                            99-089530


Editorial/production supervision: *Mary Sudul*
Cover design: *Anthony Gemmellaro*
Cover design director: *JerryVotta*
Composition: *FASTpages*
Manufacturing manager  *Maura Goldstaub*
Marketing manager: *Kate Hargett*
Acquisitions editor: *Jeffrey Pepper*

©2000 Prentice Hall PTR
Prentice-Hall, Inc.
Upper Saddle River, New Jersey 07458


Prentice Hall books are widely used by corporations and government agencies for training, marketing, and resale.

The publisher offers discounts on this book when ordered in bulk quantities. For more information, contact Corporate Sales Department, Phone: 800-382-3419; FAX: 201-236-7141; E-mail: corpsales@prenhall.com
Or write: Prentice Hall PTR, Corporate Sales Dept., One Lake Street, Upper Saddle River, NJ 07458.

Other company and product names mentioned herein are the trademarks or registered trademarks of their respective owners.

ISBN 0-13-085083-7

Printed in the United States of America
    10  9  8  7  6  5  4  3  2  1

        Prentice-Hall International (UK) Limited, *London*
        Prentice-Hall of AustraliaPty. Limited, *Sydne*
        Prentice-Hall Canada Inc., *Toronto*
        Prentice-Hall Hispanoamericana, S.A., *Mexico*
        Prentice-Hall of India Private Limited, *New Delhi*
        Prentice-Hall of Japan, Inc., *Tokyo*
        Pearson Education Asia Pte. Ltd.
        Editora Prentice-Hall do Brasil, Ltda., *Rio de Janeiro*

*"Linda, thank you for teaching me how to see.*
*You are my constant inspiration.*
*From the bottom of my heart, I will forever be yours—ilua"*

*and,*

*"Andrew, you will always be my little pumpkin."*

# Contents

# Foreword

Frank Ginac has written a book directed at the new manager, the individual accepting the reigns of leadership perhaps for the first time. In his first book, *Customer Oriented Software Quality Assurance*, Ginac addressed an important topic with a specific approach to help ensure a product result that would meet or exceed customer expectations. In *Creating High Performance Software Development Teams*, the goal is more ambitious: to provide a comprehensive vision of management for software development.

Ginac is attempting to give a template to the engineer who has achieved that milestone of transitioning from individual contributor to a member of management. For many, this may come some years after the completion of formal academic training, and in an environment offering little else in the way of support. Assuming the role of manager for the first time can be daunting, even intimidating. This book should provide some comforting guidance to successfully negotiate this challenge.

While intended for the new manager, *Creating High Performance Software Development Teams* also offers fresh insights to experienced management professionals. No matter how many years of supervising the creation of software products one has amassed, there are always new ideas or skills to acquire. Ginac has liberally relayed personal experiences into the text to make his primary points come to life.

Ginac has highlighted the undeniable importance of the planning step in software project management. Too often, this is given insufficient attention and the program ultimately suffers. It is significant as well to note that planning is not a one-time activity, but an iterative process that requires the manager's attention throughout the lifecycle of a well conceived design effort.

Team members are also singled out for their uniqueness and individuality. Software development teams are probably not best managed like athletic squads or army units; they require understanding of the engineer's nature, orientation, and objectives. In the businesses of today, fitting a management methodology to the times is appropriate, even necessary. Recognizing the speed of change and the needs of team members is essential to successfully lead the group to an on-time, on-budget and on-target product release.

So, that brings us to the topic of leadership. Ginac distinguishes between the two organizational concepts of manager and leader. It is not a given that the two are present in the same individual. But, understanding principles of leadership will allow the manager to be more complete, more likely capable of "High Performance." It is essential to be both a manager and a leader if the goals of this book are to be realized in execution.

Therefore, whether you are a new manager embarking on your first project of personal supervisory responsibility, or a veteran manager with the scars to prove it, enjoy this work as Ginac sets out to give you his prescription for *Creating High Performance Software Development Teams.*

*William G. Bock*
*September 1, 1999*

In his nearly 30 year career, William "Bill" Bock has held a number of executive level positions at TI and Convex, is the former COO of IBM/Tivoli, and is currently the president of Dazel, an H-P Software Company.

# Preface

## What Is This Book About?

This book is about creating high performance software development teams. Such teams produce superior products, on time, and on or under budget. They are not created by accident, but are created by design.

This book differs from most others like it because it focuses on the two most important elements of successful teams, people, and leadership, and then frames them within the context of a software development methodology.

It also recognizes the fact that software produced by a commercial venture is produced for a reason: to make money.

## Why Did I Write It?

I wrote this book for two reasons: to help you to be successful as a leader of software development teams and to encourage and promote the establishment of new standards by which we as members of the software development community judge the quality of the methods we use to produce software.

## Who Is This Book For?

The intended audience for this book is new or experienced software development leaders, specifically, those with software development project leadership or first level management roles and responsibilities. However, I believe that a much broader group will find this book very informative and a useful reference including middle to upper level software development managers, CEOs, presidents, and COOs of companies whose principal business is the development and sale of software products.

## Author's Bio

I think it's important for you to know a little bit about me. After all, who is this guy Frank Ginac and is he qualified to tell me how to create high performance software development teams? I graduated from Fitchburg State College in Fitchburg, Massachusetts, in 1986 with a B. S. in Computer Science. I've spent the last 13 years in the business of developing software. I've been a software test engineer, test tools developer, QA engineer, and software developer. I've lead and managed small to large teams performing each of those functions in small, medium, and large companies. My last job was vice president of product development for Dazel Corporation, recently acquired by H-P. Presently, I'm with the hottest new startup in Austin, Texas, called BroadJump, Inc. (http://www.broadjump.com) as the vice president of product development. Incidentally, both Dazel and BroadJump are Austin Ventures (http://www.austinventures.com) portfolio companies.

# Acknowledgments

## Essence of Leadership

In the pages that follow, you will learn about a style of leadership that is unlike any other—it is my style of leadership. However, I can't take credit for inventing it. Let me explain. A leadership style is like a fingerprint; on the surface, they share many characteristics, but when you look closer, each is unique. That uniqueness is a side effect of your life experiences, your interactions with the people you encounter and the events that you must deal with every day. Like every other leader, many people and events have shaped my leadership style. Foremost in my mind are a number of people who I believe have shaped it in very profound ways. They are, in effect, the essence of that style and they deserve the credit for its invention:

- Every teacher I've ever had for building the foundation.
- My Grandmother Susan Murphy for teaching me to "say it like it is."
- My cousin, Joe Tanski, for sparking my interest in computers and computer programming more than 20 years ago and for being such an amazing role model of integrity, sincerity, and generosity.
- The U.S. Army Drill Instructors of C-8-2 at Fort Jackson in Columbia, South Carolina, during the summer of 1982 for "helping" me to find my *true* limits.

- The U.S. Army R.O.T.C. Cadre at the University of Massachusetts in Amherst, Massachusetts, from 1982 through 1984 for teaching me the difference between management and leadership.
- My Pop, Tim Ginac, for teaching me all about commitment and work ethic.
- My Mom, Pat Ginac, for teaching me how to find and draw out the best in others.
- My wife, Linda Ginac, for knocking those rose-colored glasses off the end of my nose.
- My mentor and friend, Bill Bock, for teaching me how to listen.

## To Everyone Who Helped Make This Book Possible

### The Fine Folks at Prentice Hall PTR

Thank you Bernard Goodwin for publishing my first book, *Customer Oriented Software Quality Assurance*. And, thank you Jeffrey Pepper for supporting this project. Thank you to all the other folks at Prentice Hall PTR who review and edit, develop cover art, market, and sell my books.

### The Contributors

Many thanks to those who made a direct contribution to the contents of this book. Notably, Bill Bock for writing the Foreword, Matt Tormollen (vice president of marketing at BroadJump) for developing Example 1-1, the product requirements for Entropy, and C. Brad Slaten (Manager of engineering test at Dazel) for developing Example 2-3, the Hiring Profile for a senior software engineer.

### The Reviewers

Finally, many thanks to everyone who reviewed and helped me improve this manuscript. Notably, Linda Ginac, Bill Bock, Matt Chiste (co-founder of Triactive Technologies), and Steve Heller (Prentice Hall PTR).

# Introduction

## First, a Definition

What is an objective? It is a goal with an achievable and measurable end. For example, one might set an objective to lose 10 pounds by the end of the month. The goal is to lose weight and the measurable end is to lose 10 pounds by the end of the month. Is that an achievable end? Not if there is only one day left in the month! More examples of objectives include: increase revenue by 10% over the last quarter, sell more units next year than the number one competitor, and rate highest in quality among all vendors. You either achieve an objective or you don't.

## About the Examples

Throughout the book, I use examples for clarification. All of the examples describe actual events or the behaviors and actions of real people. In some cases, I've included lessons learned from experiences that I've had outside the business of software development to help clarify a particular topic. For example, I include a story from my experience teaching people how to SCUBA dive to underscore the importance of planning. I've included these stories to make the book a more interesting read. I hope that you find them informative, relevant, and entertaining.

# High Performance Versus Low Performance

## High Performance

In business, investors consider companies that consistently score high across a variety of financial metrics such as revenue growth, profitability, price-to-earnings ratio, and so on as high performers. On the other hand, marketers rate companies high performers when they own more of the market than anyone else. Still another constituency, engineers, might consider a company a high performer when it consistently releases innovative high quality products. In this book, high performance is defined as meeting or exceeding all of the objectives of a software development project. It is not sufficient to meet or exceed some of the objectives. To be a high performer, you must view a software development project as a contest that must be won. High performance then is synonymous with winning.

### Lessons from drag racing

A number of years ago, I attended a drag race for the first time at a well-known drag strip in a small New Hampshire town. As I stood waiting for the first race to begin, I could hear the deep and throaty rumble of a Chevy 454 with straight pipes approach. A black 1968 Chevy Camaro SS pulled up to the starting line ready to devour its challenger. I expected a similarly capable beast to join it, but was surprised to see a small unassuming white 1978 Chevy Chevette pull up instead. Clearly someone had made a mistake matching these two cars against each other. They edged up to the start line and revved their engines ready to spring forward. And then something that I didn't expect happened—the Chevette was given the green light and the Camaro was held at the line. A handicap! Now it all made sense.

The Chevette rolled forward straining under full throttle to get as far down the track as possible before the black beast was unleashed to chase it down. The crowd was cheering on the little car that could. When the Chevette made it about three-quarters of the way down the quarter mile track, the Camaro was unleashed. It roared down the track like a crazed dog chasing after a passing car and the crowd went wild. For the spectators, it was a classic battle of good versus evil, of little guy against big guy, of underdog against favorite. In a final burst of effort, the Chevette edged over the finish line just before the Camaro.

In the end, it didn't matter that the Camaro had a bigger engine with more horsepower than its challenger. Despite that advantage, it lost the race. Wait a minute, you might say, it was held back at the start line until the Chevette was nearly to the finish line. Didn't the Chevette have an unfair advantage? Business is much like that race; the biggest and the fastest don't always win. For that race, each driver had an objective, to win. Like that race, whether you win or lose, i.e., whether you are a high performer in business is ultimately determined by whether you meet or exceed your objectives.

### Low Performance

If you consistently achieve your objectives over time, you are viewed as a high performer. On the other hand, if you consistently fail to achieve them over time you are viewed as a low performer. It's that simple.

## Software Developers: A Unique Breed

### They Think Like Computers, if . . . then . . . else . . .

Software developers tend to view the world as if it were wrapped in a giant if-then-else statement. When faced with the challenge of solving a problem, they tend to consider only the logical elements of the problem, ignoring the emotional or human elements. That's fine when the problem being solved is inherently logical, for example, adding a new feature to a software product or fixing one of its defects. However, if the problem exists outside the realm of pure logic, then such a style of thinking often fails to find the right solution (the careful reader will notice that I've expressed this problem within an if-then construct).

Software developers routinely face problems that to solve must consider human factors. Such problems include defining and implementing a product development process, establishing effective ways to communicate, and satisfying customers. The software development leader must consider these factors as they seek the correct solution. This often places them at odds with their team because the correct solution isn't always the logical solution; this is one of the many challenges the software development leader must face.

## They Don't Like Being Told What to Do or How to Do It

One of the nice things about being a software developer is that you get a chance to use both sides of your brain. You're not an artist, a scientist, or an engineer; you're a combination of all of them. The fact that software developers do not like being told what to do, or how to do it, is a side effect of the fact that they are engaged in an activity that is sometimes right brained. A right-brained activity is one that requires creative thinking. Imagine standing over an artist's shoulder and holding on to her brush as she tries to paint her masterpiece. During right-brained activities, the software developer is much like the artist. Let me explain. In the early phase of a project, it's the right brain or creative brain working hard to understand the problem and formulate a variety of solutions. Later, after the problem is understood and a solution selected the code has to be written which, depending on whom you ask, is either a right- or left-brained activity. Next, the left brain or logical brain kicks in to deal with the more routine, predictable and mundane tasks of integration, build, test, and debug.

So, it's not that you can't tell software developers what to do or how to do it; you just have to follow a few simple rules:

- You can tell them what problem to solve (left brain).
- You can tell them to find more than one solution to the problem (left brain).
- You can't give them the solution (right brain).
- You can persuade them to implement one solution from the set that they propose (right brain, consequently you must persuade—not tell).
- You can't tell them how to write their code (right brain).
- You can tell them that they must test their code (left brain).
- You can tell them that they must fix problems in their code (left brain).

## They Are Very Curious

Curiosity leads to distraction which leads to loss of focus. If left unchecked, loss of focus leads to missing objectives and thus low performance. One malady that many software developers are afflicted with is what I call the "shiny coin chasing syndrome." I first started using this expression more than a decade ago after going to Mardi Gras in New Orleans. There, it's common for kids to make fools out of adults by placing a large, shiny coin on the ground with a transparent string attached and then yanking the coin away as the passing adults try to pick it up. A shiny coin chaser is a software developer who is easily distracted by new technologies, new and better algorithms, and the like. The Web, as fantastic a resource as it is, can exacerbate this syndrome.

## Creating High Performance Software Development Teams

By reading this book, you will learn a methodology for creating high performance software development teams that I have practiced and refined over the past 13 years. The process by which I create such teams has six major steps: (1) nail down the requirements, (2) build the best team, (3) prepare the team, (4) prepare to lead, (5) plan, and (6) execute with passion. Chapters 1 through 6 of this book correspond to each of these steps.

You might be wondering why a book about creating high performance software development teams devotes only one chapter to building the team and five chapters to requirements, training, planning, and the like. Bringing together a group of people and calling them a team doesn't make them a team and doesn't guarantee any particular outcome. High performance teams, either through training or experience, recognize this and perform all of the steps listed above, but sometimes with variations in order. One popular variation is to swap Steps 1 and 2. Another is to follow Step 1 with Step 5 and then with Steps 2, 3, 4, and 6. Following the steps in the order I've laid them out has worked the best for me. Over time, as you repeatedly apply these steps to projects that you lead, you will find an order that works best for you. Let's take a look at each step in greater detail.

### Nail Down the Requirements

Requirements must answer some basic questions: What problem will the product solve? How will the product solve the problem? Who has the problem? When do they need a solution? Finally, is it worth building? The answers to these questions form the foundation upon which everything else that follows is built: building the team, preparing the team, planning, and execution. Just like a house is only as good as its foundation, a software product is only as good as its requirements. Chapter 1 explores each question above in depth, explores ways to get the answers, considers an all-too-often ignored subject called innovation, and culminates with an example of a requirements document that you can use as a model.

## Build the Best Team

How do you build a high performance software development team when its members think like computers, don't like being told what to do or how to do it, and are curious and often stray from their objectives? Start by hiring the best talent that you can afford.

Don't approach hiring as if it were a numbers game, a slot-filling exercise, or a race against time. You will achieve much better results if you focus on hiring people that match your needs rather than simply hiring to fill an opening in your organizational chart or hiring to beat a hiring deadline. In Chapter 2, you'll learn how to create a hiring profile that defines your ideal candidate across four dimensions: (1) cultural fit, (2) personality, (3) track record, and (4) knowledge, skills, and experience. You'll also learn how to find that person, determine if they are a fit, sell them on your organization, make them an offer, and close the deal.

The way your team is organized also plays a crucial role in whether it is successful. Traditional organizational structures aren't optimized for high performance. There is a better way. And, you'll learn what it is in Chapter 2.

## Prepare the Team

If our world were ideal, you'd always find people that exactly match the profile of the person that you're looking for. More often than not, they have too much or not enough of what you're looking for. At a minimum, to create a high performance software development team, you must hire someone who is a close cultural and personality match with your hiring profile and who has a solid track record of accomplishment. A mismatch there cannot be corrected. If the holes in their knowledge, skills, and experience fall within the parameters of your profile, they can be filled in. Chapter 3 explains how to identify and fill in those holes.

## Prepare to Lead

To effectively lead a team, you must remember that you are leading people. People are complex, far more complex than the most sophisticated machines ever devised. Treat them like machines and you will achieve suboptimal results. In Chapter 4, you'll learn how to look at your team as a group of people not as resources.

There is a difference between leading and managing. Leading people is fundamentally about pulling them toward their objectives. Managing people is about pushing them there. High performance teams are lead not managed. Are you a manager or a leader? Chapter 4 will help you figure that out. If you're not a leader, you'll learn how to become one.

## Plan

Planning is boring to software developers. They want to design and code. To make matters worse, operating without a plan, by the seat of your pants, adds an element of risk and excitement to a project that appeals to many software developers, particularly those with a strong entrepreneurial spirit.

The worst case is no plan at all. Lacking any objectives such projects are doomed to fail. The next best case is a plan that enumerates objectives but does not lay out a clear and well-thought-out course that maps how to get from where you are to where you want to go. Next is a proper plan with objectives and a well designed course that isn't followed. Finally, there's the proper plan that is followed. The last case is the one that leads to the consistent achievement of objectives, and consequently, high performance.

One common misconception about planning that frustrates most novice project planners is that planning is an exact science; in other words, it's possible to produce a plan that is 100% accurate. Unfortunately, and for a variety of reasons, project planning is inherently imprecise. It is very common for novice planners to invest a tremendous amount of time building what they think is a precise and accurate plan only to be disappointed later when they fail to meet the project's objectives. Many conclude from such an experience that planning is a waste of time and they regress to the seat-of-the-pants method. Planning is best approached following an 80/20 rule; aim for 80% accuracy in the first cut of the plan and refine it toward 100% during execution. In Chapter 5, you'll learn how to plan and execute a project following this rule.

## Execute With Passion

Nailing down the requirements, hiring the right talent, organizing for success, preparing your team, learning how to lead, and planning culminates with execution. All of the hard work that went into getting to this point can easily be undone. How do you prevent that from happening?

You have a plan, *follow it*. I'm always amazed when I see someone put tremendous effort into getting to this point only to ignore their plan during execution. In the end, it's all about execution. The plan is your roadmap. Use it. In Chapter 6, you'll learn how to work your plan.

I'll never forget the feedback a former manager of mine gave me during an annual review early in my career; he said, "Frank, you care too much." I made the mistake of taking his feedback to heart and attempted to care less. Eventually, though, I regressed. I couldn't help but care deeply about what I was doing, what we were doing as a team, and the company's success. Do not allow the emotional momentum that has built up to fizzle out during execution. In addition to learning how to work your plan, in Chapter 6, you'll learn about the things you must do to maintain that momentum—to execute with passion.

## Software Development

One assumption that the first six chapters of this book makes is that you are familiar with the subject of software development. For those readers who are not, and for those who are but want my thoughts on the subject, I've included information about software development in the Appendix. Skip there and then come back to Chapter 1 if you want to fill in a hole. The material from the chapter was borrowed from my book *Customer Oriented Software Quality Assurance.*[*]

---

[*] Ginac, Frank P. *Customer Oriented Software Quality Assurance.* Prentice Hall PTR. Englewood Cliffs, NJ: 1997.

# Nail Down the Requirements

## Purpose of Requirements

Chances are you live far enough from your office that you need to use some form of transportation to get there. Your options may include motorcycles, buses, subways, car pools, or a car. Why own a car if your transportation needs can be satisfied by cycling to work or taking the bus? You may want the greater degree of freedom and control that owning and driving your own car provides. Why not a bicycle instead of an expensive automobile? You may not want to exert the physical effort or expend the time it would take to pedal to work. Why not own a basic automobile that gets you to your office in a reasonable amount of time? You may want one that lets others know something about your personality, or one that reflects your personal financial status, and the like. Notice that I used the words "need" and "want" above. Need refers to a lower order cognitive void that you feel a strong desire to fill. Want refers to a higher order cognitive preference for how to fill that void.

The degree to which people both need and want something determines its value, i.e., what they're willing to pay for it. Determining the value of something is referred to as pricing. There are many pricing strategies: guessing, pricing below the competition, charging a premium for a top-of-the-line product, and others. Regardless of which strategy you choose for a particular product, the price people pay must produce a profitable result, or eventually you'll go out of business.

Our challenge as software development professionals is to satisfy our customers' needs and wants with software products that they are willing to pay enough for to make it profitable for us. How can we be sure that what we are building accomplishes that objective? At the root of a customer's need is a problem to be solved. The way in which it is solved should be driven by what they want. For example, imagine a customer of yours who needs to solve the problem of communicating with their field personnel. They could solve the problem using a telephone. However, they believe that effective communication involves "seeing" the person with whom they are communicating. They want a solution that allows both parties to talk to and see each other. The problem to be solved, i.e., communicate with field personnel, coupled with a desirable solution to that problem, i.e., the ability to see the other person, forms a requirement for the product. Requirements must answer some basic questions:

- What problem will the product solve, i.e., do they need it?
- How will the product solve the problem, i.e., do they want it?
- Who has the problem, and how many have the problem?
- When do they need a solution?
- Finally, is it worth building?

## The Questions

The answers to the questions below will be used to build the requirements document for a product. At the end of this chapter is an example of such a document. The easiest way to remember what questions must be answered is to remember the acronym POWRR for Problem, Opportunity, Window, Return, and Requirements.

### Problem

#### What problem will the product solve?

Give a team of software developers a whiteboard and a marker, remove the constraints of time, money, resources, and requirements, and they'll conjure up an endless supply of new and often very interesting products. Occasionally, they'll create something that the world has never seen before, but everybody wants. More often than not, such inventions fail to proliferate and endure. Fundamentally, this happens for one of two reasons: (1) nobody knows about the product, or (2) they know about it but don't need or want it. The former can be resolved through an effective marketing program. The latter can be resolved by knowing your customers' needs and building products that they want. There are three permutations of needs and wants: (1) nobody needs your product, therefore nobody wants it, (2) somebody needs your product but nobody wants it, and (3) somebody needs your product and they want it.

### *Wrong problem (lacks need), unwanted solution*

History is replete with examples of inventions that simply satisfy no apparent need. I qualified the word "need" in the last sentence with the word "apparent" because people don't always recognize how something satisfies one of their needs. At the heart of every purchase decision is the intrinsic question, "Does this satisfy some need?" The solution is irrelevant if the answer to that question is negative. If you have a product that satisfies no need, but are compelled to sell it anyway, hire the best marketing and sales professionals you can. Marketing professionals will craft a need and determine how to convince you that you must satisfy that need. Sales professionals will figure out how to get you to ignore this question and buy the product whether you need it or not.

### *Right problem (needed), unwanted solution*

In the office building where I used to work, there's a display that houses models of "washing machines" from the turn of the Twentieth Century on loan from the U.S. Patent Office. There are machines that twist the clothes, some that press them, and still others that spin or agitate them. All of them probably do a fine job of cleaning clothes, which is the problem they were clearly designed to solve, but only the last types have survived the test of time. Why? Lurking behind the obvious problem, the need to clean clothes, was the real problem: washing clothes by hand is time intensive manual labor, i.e., hard work. The other machines didn't do enough to make the task of washing clothes easier. Each piece of clothing had to be processed one-at-a-time, by hand. With the latter, all the clothes could be washed at the same time, hands-free. Add a motor, and you had an unattended hands-free clothes washer; the solution that everyone favored.

### *Right problem (needed), wanted solution—a winning product!*

Like most professionals, I have too much to do and a calendar more complex than my brain can maintain on its own. To solve this problem, i.e., extend my brain's capacity to remember, I started using a time honored memory enhancing tool known as a piece of paper and a pencil. But, I'm a technologist and technologists simply cannot use such primitive instruments. In other words, my need was satisfied with paper and pencil, but I wanted a technology-based solution. I found a software package that I could run on my PC and that appeared to satisfy my need in a way I wanted to have it satisfied.

Once I transferred everything from paper to this software package, I became a slave to my computer. I had to go back to my office every time I needed to refresh my brain or change my schedule. My other option was to carry my computer around with me, but that was impractical because it was too heavy and awkward to carry around, and I needed to be plugged in to the network to synchronize my calendar with the master calendar stored on one of our servers. I suppose I could have solved those problems by buying a sub-notebook or handheld computer and convincing my company to invest in wireless networking technology. But that would have been too expensive.

Some former colleagues, product marketers of course, started bringing in these tiny computers called PDAs or Personal Data Assistants to manage their schedules. I'm sure you've seen them; they have no keyboard, a tiny low resolution monochrome display, and a primitive operating system and applications. You enter input using a stylus and write in a kind of script called Graffiti. How could such a device, clearly a technological back step, with the exception that you enter input by writing instead of typing, be of any use to anyone? Yet, despite these apparent limitations, they all seemed hooked on this technology. One of my colleagues allowed me a test drive. Within minutes, I too was hooked. I found a superior solution to my original problem; it is based on technology, it is portable, and by adding a wireless modem, I could synchronize with the master calendar wherever I happened to be. I would also be able to send and receive e-mail and browse the Web without having to go back to my office or tether myself to a telephone line or network port.

At that point, I simply had to have one. Thanks to my wonderful wife who bought me a PDA for my last birthday, I do. I can't imagine how I ever got along without it. I also can't imagine ever going back to using paper and pencil. But the truth is, paper and pencil solved the original problem, to maintain my calendar. I moved to a technology-based solution because I wanted to, not because I needed to, which led to the creation of two new problems. I could have solved the two new problems by falling back to the previous solution. However, I chose to solve them by purchasing a new gadget. Why? Because that was what I wanted and felt I needed.

## Opportunity

### Who has the problem?

One of the biggest mistakes you can make is to assume that your customers are just like you. Make that assumption and you will surely build a product that is too difficult for them to install, use, and maintain. It will have features they don't want and it will be missing ones that they desperately need. The bottom line is that you must get to know them. You must know them well enough to describe them as if you were describing a close friend or family member. You must then use that description to help shape the requirements for your product.

Dazel develops business critical software for large global enterprises. Business critical is another way of saying that if the software stops working, the part of their customers' business that depends on that software comes to a screeching halt. Such interruptions result in significant losses in productivity, revenue, and the like. Needless to say, the companies that buy their software have a very low tolerance for such interruptions. When I was with Dazel, in the early versions of the product we looked at uptime from our perspective (uptime is the amount of time between an unintended or forced shutdown). For us, although we used our own product internally, we didn't use it in the business critical way of our customers. When the system failed, we restarted it. Since such failures happened infrequently, it was relatively easy to restart the system, and it caused little disruption to our business, it seemed a reasonable flaw to live with. We were wrong and learned a painful lesson; never assume that what's good for the goose is good for the gander. Fortunately, we were able to correct the problem and survived our mistake.

### How many have the problem?

The universe of people who have the problem and are candidate buyers of a solution is referred to as the market. Before you decide whether to solve the problem, i.e., build your product, you must know how many prospective buyers of your solution there are. For a well-defined market, consulting an industry analyst group such as Forrester, IDG, Gartner, or Giga is an excellent way to determine market size. For a new or emerging market, sizing the market is a bit more difficult. Experts tell me that to size such markets they simply venture a guess.

## Window of Opportunity

### When do they need a solution?

Have you ever heard expressions like "Timing is everything" or "He received that promotion because he was in the right place at the right time?" For software product development, timing may not be everything, but it certainly rates highly. To the person experiencing the problem that your product will someday solve, the availability of a solution is important. They may need a solution immediately or they might be willing to wait. Regardless, they want to know when the solution will be available. Timing also plays a crucial role in assessing the strength of the need. If there's no urgency around filling that need, chances are that it is not very strong. In other words, demand is weak. Weak demand means that you won't likely sell many units and you will be unable to command a premium for each unit.

It has been my experience that whatever date you come up with, it will be too late. It might be too late for a particular customer or prospect, i.e., they need or want a solution right now, or it might be too late for the market, i.e., a competitor is poised to beat you to market and establish itself as the market leader. The speed with which you can release a solution is constrained by a variety of factors. Some constraints are easy to observe and measure, e.g., the completion of a product may be dependent on the completion of another product. Others are a bit more difficult to see, e.g., hitting a market window of opportunity. The following sections explore some of those factors.

### *Date driven by the completion of another product*

Dependency relationships come in a variety of forms that we'll examine in much greater detail later in the book. In this case, your ability to release a product depends on another project finishing. This is perhaps the most common of the timing related factors.

### *Market window of opportunity*

There are countless stories of companies that have produced products that are superior to their competitions', but were second or third to market allowing their competitors to gain a majority of the market share. Once you're behind, it's difficult to catch up to and then pass your competitors. After someone else owns a market, it can be difficult if not impossible to unseat them from their lead position. But not always. Again, it often comes back to timing. Once a company owns a market, it must stay ahead of the competition; otherwise over time, its market share will erode. Staying ahead of the competition is fundamentally a matter of timing.

## Return

### Is the product worth building?

Effective marketing and sales professionals either exploit real or imagined needs and wants, or they create them. Next, they figure out how much someone will pay to satisfy those needs and wants. It's possible that although someone has a need they're not willing to pay much, if anything, to satisfy it. In that case, it may not be worth it for you to develop a product that satisfies that need. To determine whether a product is worth building, you must develop a business case. The simplest such case is to anticipate a product's return.

### What is ROI?

ROI stands for Return on Investment. It is a simple financial measure that can be used to determine whether some venture is worth the investment. There are more sophisticated measures such as Net Present Value and Internal Rate of Return, but I have found that a simple ROI calculation that uses a healthy fudge factor does a good job of determining whether an investment in a particular product development effort will produce a positive return over that product's lifetime. Put simply, if it looks like you're going to put more in than you get out, then the investment is not likely worthwhile. Conversely, if it looks like you're going to get more out than you put in, the venture is probably worth investing in.

### Calculating ROI

The formula for calculating ROI is simple:

*Gross ROI* = Number of Prospects * Conversion Rate * Avg. Price per Sale

*Net ROI* = Gross ROI − ((Cost to Build + Cost of Sales) * 10)

where,

- **Number of Prospects** is the total number of buyers most likely to purchase the product, i.e., it solves a problem they have in a way they find appealing.
- **Conversion Rate** is the percentage of those prospects that you anticipate will actually purchase the product.
- **Average Price per Sale** is simply the average price you believe each prospect will pay for the product.
- **Cost to Build** includes all expenses that you will incur over the lifetime of the product. The largest expenses associated with the development of software products tends to be the total of all salaries paid and overhead, i.e., benefits, taxes, and such, to the people that design, implement, and test the product over its lifetime. It also includes tangible capital expenses such as hardware, software licenses, and the like.
- **Cost of Sales** are the expenses incurred to market, sell, and support the product over its lifetime.
- **10** is the fudge factor. In other words, it accounts for the fact that all other factors in the equation are inaccurate. It has worked well for me, but whether or not **10** is the right number for you is something that you'll have to determine over time.

## Requirements

### How will the product solve the problem?

An effective requirements document communicates specific features and capabilities that a product must possess. And it explicitly maps those features and capabilities back to the problem to be solved. It does not contain items that don't in some way contribute to the solution. Upon reading such a document, the reader should have a clear picture of the problem to be solved and all of the things that must be done to solve that problem. It does not contain extraneous features and capabilities.

### How will customers use the product?

The best way to describe your customer is to describe how they will use your product. One way to do that is through Use Cases. The other is through Customer Scenarios.

#### Use Cases

A Use Case describes a single start-to-finish or front-to-back application of a product. For example, the word processor that I'm using to write this book can be used to develop a variety of documents from simple memos to complex multi-part documents. In some cases, this product might be used to create a simple document that is printed, while in other cases it might be used to create a complex document that is e-mailed. In yet another case, it might be used to create a simple document that is exported as text and then included as an embedded or linked object in other applications.

As you can see, there are countless ways in which this product can be used. The idea behind Use Cases is to define a set of cases that collectively represent the most common ways the product is to be used. They are used to shape the design and implementation of the product as well as the way that it is tested and qualified. Here, I'm using the term "tested" to mean that the product has been verified to work as designed and the term "qualified" to mean that the product has been certified to work properly in a customer environment.

#### Customer Scenarios

A Customer Scenario can be thought of as a combination of Use Cases applied repeatedly over some period of time. For example, a database server is used to store data in tables. The data is then used either directly by an end-user through an ad hoc or predefined query or it is used by an application. There may be peaks and valleys with respect to the number of users simultaneously accessing the database, the volume of data they are retrieving or storing, and the complexity of their queries. Administrators may use a variety of utilities to monitor the database server to make sure it is functioning properly. They may also routinely execute utilities that clean up or reorganize the database. Implicit in this example is a time line.

Like Use Cases, Customer Scenarios, when collected together, are used to shape the design and implementation of the product as well as the way in which it is tested and qualified.

## Getting the Answers

### Customers and Prospects

What better way is there to understand your customers' requirements than by calling them, visiting them, and sending them questionnaires. Unless you employ some method of collecting requirements from them directly, you are either assuming or guessing.

Like your customers, you must collect prospects' requirements directly. The methods that you use to collect their requirements are the same as those you use to collect them from your customers.

### Competitors

Creating requirements that are derived from analyzing your competitors' products is a bit more difficult. They are not likely to answer your calls, allow you to visit them, sell their products to you, or respond to your questionnaires. Other methods must be employed.

## Develop a Theme for the Project (Keep It Simple)

The project theme articulates the purpose of the project in a clear, concise, and memorable way. In other words, the theme is a summary statement of the requirements. A well-written project theme is easier to memorize than a list of requirements. Because it is memorable, it helps to keep the project team focused.

In fact, you should ask your team to memorize the theme. Tell them that everything they do should be measured against the project theme. For example, let's say that the theme is to improve performance. One day, while working on a performance enhancement task, one of your developers discovers an opportunity to rewrite a section of code that will make it easier to someday localize the product. Should they take the time to perform this extra task? Since it has nothing to do with the theme of the project, the answer is no. Another advantage of having a project theme is apparent from the example above; the developer was empowered to make the decision.

To make a project theme memorable, keep it simple and relate it to something that your team can easily identify with. One way to construct a memorable theme is to include a backgrounder. I originally heard of this idea from a former colleague. The idea is borrowed from the movie industry. There, backgrounders are used to establish a context for a movie, i.e., set the stage for the story. For software development projects, backgrounders can be used to establish the context for the project. It answers the question, "Why are we building this?"

## Temper Requirements with Innovation

This part of the requirements definition process is all too often ignored. There are countless examples of companies that rise to the top of their market (indeed they may have even created the market) through innovation and then abandon the practice of innovation when they reach the top. One of the best ways to remain at the top of a market is to constantly redefine the market through innovation. Through innovation, you constantly change the rules, making it difficult if not impossible for others to "catch up" and displace you. If you're not currently at the top, use innovation to unseat those that have abandoned the practice. Use it to generate interest. Use it to create excitement and enthusiasm in the marketplace. Use it to discourage your competitors.

## Example 1–1: Product Requirements Document

### Product Requirements

### 1.0 PRODUCT NAME/RELEASE

Entropy v2.0

### 2.0 RELEASE THEME

The purpose of this release is to enable successful customer enterprise deployments of Entropy by attacking a major product shortcoming, product reliability.

### 3.0 DEFINE THE MARKET

### 3.1 Problem

The theme of Entropy v1.0 was to deliver a feature-rich product to market at least 90 days ahead of the competition. Quality was compromised to meet these objectives. As a result, many of our customers have had poor early experiences with the product. In particular, many have experienced significant problems while attempting to deploy the product across their respective enterprises.

### 3.2 Opportunity

#### 3.2.1 Buyer Profile

The target buyer of Entropy is the IT professional managing the corporate IT department at a mid-market company where mid-market is defined to be all companies with annual revenues between $500M and $1.5B.

#### 3.2.2 Number of Buyers

Based on information reported by International Market Alchemists, there are approximately 1,000 prospective buyers of Entropy.

### 3.3 Window of Opportunity

By plotting the erosion of our market share caused by the entrance of new competitors that are entering the market at an alarming rate and factoring in the loss of many key sales opportunities to competitors due to product shortcomings, we will lose our position as market leader within six months. We believe that if Entropy v2.0 is released within the next 90 days, combined with an aggressive marketing campaign and pricing, we will render newer competitors ineffective and will maintain our leadership position.

### 4.0 RETURN ON INVESTMENT

*Gross ROI* = 1,000 prospects * 50% conversion * $150,000.00
*Net ROI*  = $75M − (($1.5M + $0.75M) * *10*)
       = $52.5M

### 5.0 REQUIREMENTS

### 5.1 Product Requirements

(In priority order)

1. Improve the reliability of the Entropy servers by increasing mean time between failure from one week to 16 weeks.
2. Further improve the reliability of Entropy servers by reducing the number of defects related to servers crashing, hanging, dumping core, and disappearing by 25%.

Example 1–1: Product Requirements Document 13

3. Reduce the number of defects related to the loss of operational data within the system by eliminating those defects involving general system failures.
4. Improve the performance of key operations by 200%.
5. Ensure that Entropy is Y2K compliant.

### 5.2 Documentation Requirements

1. Update existing publications to reflect product modifications.
2. Develop a new publication that describes information and error codes returned by Entropy.
3. Document with the assistance of Customer Support, Professional Services, Field Support, and Marketing, "Enterprise Deployment Best Practices." The goal of documenting "Best Practices" will be to mitigate known limitations concerning enterprise deployment. Examples include replication strategies, fail-over strategies, and service monitoring strategies.

### 5.3 Quality Assurance and Testing Requirements

1. Certify the release on the following platforms:
   Tier 1
   - Microsoft Windows NT 4.0 Service Pack 5—Server Edition and Enterprise Edition on Intel using NTFS
   - Sun Solaris 7 on Sparc
   - IBM AIX 4.3.2 on RS/6000
   - HP/UX 10.20
   Tier 2
   - HP/UX 11.0 on PA-RISC, 32-bit only
2. Design and implement customer scenario tests based on the following customers:
   - Jones' Pet Foods
   - Drugs R Us
   - Sisters Power Company
   - Metalman Industrial Products
3. Design and implement the following classes of use cases:
   - End-user client installation and configuration
   - Basic end-user operations

- Advanced end-user operations
- Basic Help Desk user operations
- Advanced Help Desk user operations
- Administrative user server installation and configuration
- Administrative user routine server maintenance operations
- Administrative user server operations

4. Collect performance characterization data as a goal of the quality assurance process.

## 6.0 DEPENDENCIES

1. Acquisition and implementation of requisite hardware and software to develop and test the product.
2. Staffing to plan in Engineering, Test, Tech Pubs, and Quality Assurance.

# CHAPTER 2

# Build the Best Team

## Piecing Together the Puzzle

Building the best team is like putting together a puzzle where the pieces for the puzzle that you are building are all mixed in with the pieces from other puzzles.

### Define the Team's Objectives

A common mistake that many software development managers make is to assume that an arbitrary collection of software developers makes a team, and that all such teams can achieve whatever objectives are placed before them. This is simply not true. The profession we practice is not unlike the legal and medical professions in that although members of each profession may share some basic knowledge and skills, the breadth and depth of knowledge and skills required to practice all forms of law and medicine far exceed the capacity of any individual. Consequently, those professions, like ours, are segmented into specialties.

In assembling the team, you must know what you want that team to accomplish before you select its members (refer to Chapter 1). If the team's objective will be to design and implement a new operating system, then you'll need to select software developers who have the requisite knowledge and skills needed to be successful in such a project. On the other hand, if the objective of the team will be to develop a financial analysis tool for stock brokers, the knowledge and skills they'll need will be far different from those required by the operating system development team. Remember, software developers are not interchangeable parts.

## Hiring Profile

After you define what you want the team to do, the next step in building the best team is to create a hiring profile consisting of four categories:

1. Culture
2. Personality
3. Track record
4. Knowledge, skills, and experience

To help you recall them, remember the acronym CaPTain K. Each category should have objective requirements. In the following sections, we'll examine each of these in greater detail ending with an example of a hiring profile.

### Culture

***What is culture?***

Culture is the common set of beliefs and values that a body of people shares. Corporate culture is the culture of a company. There are always two sides to a company's corporate culture. One side is the one that the company wants its employees, prospective new hires, and the public in general to see; its persona. The other is its true culture, the culture its employees practice everyday. There are always differences between the two. Problems arise when the gap is wide. Hiring plays a key role in preventing that from happening. By hiring people that are a close match to the stated culture, chances are high that the gap will be small.

***What is your company's culture?***

Grab a piece of paper and a pencil (or your PDA) and write down the top three or four values and beliefs espoused by your company's topmost leaders, i.e., your president and the members of her staff. After you've done that, repeat the exercise but base what you write down on your observations, not on what you've read in a memo produced by your HR department and signed by your president. Are the lists identical? Close? Or, grossly divergent? Figure 2-1 is an example of a company culture that is in reality congruent with its stated culture:

**Figure 2-1**

| Statement of Corporate Culture | Reality |
|---|---|
| 1. Produce highest quality products. | 1. Products never released until all tests pass. |
| 2. Satisfy customers. | 2. Planned work is halted to tackle tough customer problems. |
| 3. Maintain market leadership. | 3. Continuous product innovations planned for and released ahead of competition. |
| 4. Practice focus and intensity. | 4. Everyone operates heads down—very little cooler talk. |
| 5. Work as a team. | 5. Everyone asks, "What can I do to help?" Nobody says, "It's not my job!" Nobody sees their job as more important than anyone else's. |

Figure 2-2 is an example of a company culture that is in reality grossly divergent from its stated culture:

**Figure 2-2**

| Statement of Corporate Culture | Reality |
|---|---|
| 1. Produce highest quality products. | 1. Products routinely released to meet schedule without completing testing or passing all tests. |
| 2. Satisfy customers. | 2. Customer problems go unresolved for weeks or months to work on "more important" tasks. |
| 3. Maintain market leadership. | 3. Products outdated. |
| 4. Practice focus and intensity. | 4. Most people spend half their day surfing the Web. |
| 5. Work as a team. | 5. Everyone says, "It's not my job!" Certain people view their jobs as more important than others. |

### Is it what you'd like it to be?

If your company's culture is what you want it to be, then keep doing what you must be doing: hiring people who are close cultural fits. On the other hand, if your culture needs improvement, change it by hiring those that personify the culture you wish to create.

Let's say that in your present culture, people have fallen into the habit of blaming others for their failures. You want to change the culture to one where people accept responsibility for their failures. You recognize that this particular aspect of your culture was created by the departing manager whose replacement you are hiring. That manager would publicly humiliate people by drawing attention to their mistakes and failures. His subordinates found that by blaming someone else, they could avoid public embarrassment and humiliation, i.e., they found a way to avoid the pain.

During interviews, you meet with two candidates who appear to fit. But, since changing this aspect of your culture is important, you ask probing questions to determine how each would handle mistakes and failures. You find that one of the candidates would most likely embarrass his subordinates and the other would encourage them to openly discuss their failures and look for ways to prevent them from happening again. All else being equal, which candidate would you choose?

### Personality

### Needs to be as close to perfect as possible—this is a gap that you cannot close

Remember from the Introduction that a high performance team is one that consistently meets or exceeds *all* of its objectives. Personality plays a key role. A person who is laid back and carefree may not be concerned about getting a release out on time. Another person who dislikes change and who passively resists it may not look for ways to improve the efficiency of (or bypass) a process to pull in the date on a slipping project.

The behaviors associated with personality are deeply rooted. They are connected to an internal belief system that often reaches back to early childhood. Their connection with deeply rooted beliefs makes such behaviors difficult, if not impossible, to change. Other behaviors aren't as deeply rooted. They're more like habits. Not necessarily easy to change, but possible. In either case, if you knew before hiring a person, that they possessed certain personality qualities that were at odds with your goal to create a high performance team, would you hire that person?

If you hire someone who exhibits personality traits that are at odds with the kind of traits characteristic of a high performance team member, you will most certainly end up firing that person someday. Or, you'll spend a tremendous amount of time counseling and couching that person attempting to change those behaviors, i.e., attempting to close the gap between what they are and what you need them to be. Is that the best use of your time? If you answered yes, you might have chosen the wrong career.

### *Track record of being...*

In my experience, high performers consistently possess certain qualities, including:

#### *Self-starters/Initiators*

They are people who need little if any coaxing to take action. They see what needs to be done and do it.

#### *Risk takers*

They are the risk takers not the risk averse. This behavior spills over into their personal lives. They engage in high risk activities such as mountain biking, rock climbing, skydiving, and the like.

#### *Unhappy with the status quo/Change drivers*

They are always looking to improve the way things are done and they are always looking to improve themselves. Beyond looking, they are effective at affecting change. They have track records of introducing new processes or changing ones that don't work. They are avid readers, have mentors, and take training classes.

#### *Ambitious*

They are always seeking more responsibility and opportunities for growth. They won't be held back. They are race horses not mules.

#### *Leaders*

When the going gets tough, they rise up and lead the way. They're the ones that people follow regardless of their formal position within the corporate hierarchy.

### Track record

How do you determine if the person whose resume you're looking at has what you're looking for? Look for the resume that is achievement oriented. In other words, look for the resume that identifies the successful application of knowledge, skills, and experience versus boasting about possessing certain knowledge, skills, and experience. For example, results-oriented high performers will list things like, "Designed and implemented an engineering process that improved the accuracy of project scheduling by over 90%" on their resume. On the other hand, a non-results oriented person may only list items on their resume like, "Attended project management training." Example 2-1 shows a resume that says very little about results. It talks of titles, responsibilities, and the like. Example 2-2, however, goes further by enumerating significant accomplishments.

## Example 2-1

**JOHN E. BRAVO**
100 Activity Lane • Spinning, Texas • 78000
H: (512) 555-1212 • W: (512) 555-1212

**OBJECTIVE**
    An executive level engineering management position

**PROFESSIONAL EXPERIENCE**
    **ANDREW'S CORPORATION** • 1996 to Present
    Austin, Texas
    *Vice President of Product Development*: Corporate Officer and Manager of Product Development Department consisting of 50 professionals. Responsible for sustaining and evolving all existing products and developing all new products. Manage an operating and capital budget in excess of 3 million dollars.
      • Hire/Develop engineering management staff
      • Plan and manage engineering budget, both personnel and capital
      • Design and implement engineering-wide processes and procedures
      • Work closely with marketing to define product requirements
      • Member of strategic product planning committee responsible for defining short- and long-term product strategy

**EDUCATION**
    BS COMPUTER SCIENCE, 1986
    Small Northeast College - Fitchburg, Massachusetts

**PROFESSIONAL TRAINING**
    Leadership and Teamwork • Supervising Technical Professionals

# Example 2-2

**JOHN E. QUEST**
100 Achievement Drive • Leader, Texas • 78000
H: (512) 555-1212 • W.: (512) 555-1212

**OBJECTIVE: EXECUTIVE-LEVEL ENGINEERING MANAGEMENT**
To lead the Engineering Department in a leading-edge high technology start-up company by contributing proven ability to:
• Provide leadership in organizing operations, building high-performance teams, and generating profitable ideas
• Create and release successful new products and releases utilizing in-depth knowledge of company's marketspace and customer requirements
• Simultaneously manage multiple development projects through the design and development of engineering processes and procedures

**QUALIFICATIONS:** A self-motivated engineering professional with over 14 years experience with a reputation for:

| | | |
|---|---|---|
| • Operations/Business Planning | • High-quality Processes | • Strong Team Player |
| • Management/Leadership | • Planning and Project Execution | • Outstanding Communication |
| • Engineering Excellence | • Project Management | • Achieving Outstanding Results |

**ACHIEVEMENTS:**
DEVELOPED the first Widget system which sold tenfold the investment in the first year following its release.
CREATED and DIRECTED product development teams for a start-up company. Planned, developed, managed and measured over a dozen new product releases, a number of major upgrades, and many third-party integration packages.
INNOVATED and IMPLEMENTED processes to improve product quality and significantly increase time-to-market resulting in robust, high-quality software developed in shorter development cycles.

**PROFESSIONAL EXPERIENCE:**
*Vice President of Product Development*   Andrew's Corporation, Austin, Texas, 1996 to Present
Developed the world's first Widget system. Responsible for developing and sustaining all existing Big Company's products, definition of product strategy, hiring and developing the engineering management team, and development of engineering budgets. Manage a direct staff of 5 and extended staff of 45 professionals. Have held positions as *Director of Engineering* and *Manager of Business Response Team.*
• Managed development of a number of releases of the Widget Server including major, minor, and maintenance releases - evolved product from a feature deficient, unreliable, unscalable application to a robust, dependable, enterprise scalable application
• Managed the development of various integration packages including Widget for ERP, and Widget for ESM
• Managed development of several major releases of the Widget for ERP integration option - gained certification through ERP vendor
• Managed maintenance of all Widget for ESM integration products originally developed by Big Company's consulting organization

**EDUCATION:**
BS Computer Science
Graduated with HONORS, 1986
Small Northeast College - Fitchburg, Massachusetts

## Knowledge, skills, and experience needed for success

There are software developers who specialize in the development of standalone applications for certain professions like medical or legal. Others specialize in the development of software for banking and finance. Some develop real-time control system software. Still others have built careers developing client-server middleware used by others to build sophisticated client-server applications for a variety of professions and industries. Each has unique knowledge, skills, and experience that don't easily, if at all, transfer from one kind of software development project to another.

### *Doesn't need to be a perfect match, but the gap between their skills and your needs should be narrow*

It is rare to find someone who is a perfect match with the profile you create of the ideal candidate. It is useful to specify what skills and experience candidates must possess and those that are strongly desired but you can live without, at least on a temporary basis. If they are things that you can live without permanently, don't put them on the list. For the temporary ones, you'll have to determine how long and how much effort it will take you to help that person fill those holes. If the gap between what they have and what you need is narrow, then it's probably a reasonable risk to hire that person, but a risk nonetheless. A wide gap means longer time to fill and more effort on your part. How many such projects can you afford to take on and maintain your performance as the team's leader?

When you hire them, and assuming they accept, identify the gaps that you see. Work with them to develop a detailed plan to close those gaps. Don't ignore them. What might be a narrow gap today could easily become a wide one if left unchecked.

### *Correlation between university degree and performance*

I hate to admit it, because I'm a big fan of getting a university education, but I've found no correlation between having a university degree and one's performance. Some of the best and brightest high performers I've ever worked with have had no degree or have degrees in other completely unrelated fields. On second thought, perhaps there is a correlation: those who have no degree or a degree in an unrelated field are more likely to be high performance team members than those who do.

I'm not suggesting that you hire only people who have no degree or a degree in an unrelated field. What I am suggesting is that if you are prejudiced toward hiring only people with computer science degrees, drop your prejudice. You're passing over candidates who in many cases will bring you a greater return than those with a degree.

# Example 2-3

## Example Hiring Profile:
## Hiring Profile for Senior Software Engineers

### CULTURE

The ideal candidates will be a close cultural fit. This is essential to both preserve the culture and to maximize the candidates' productivity and likelihood for success. The ideal candidates will possess the following cultural attributes:

- **Commitment to excellence**
The company values people who take great pride in their work and are committed to producing only the finest results. It also values people who vigorously defend their commitment to excellence by standing up and challenging decisions that compromise excellence.

- **Can-do attitude**
The company values people who make every effort to achieve their goals and objectives regardless of how difficult or challenging those goals and objectives may be.

- **Strong desire to win**
The company values people who understand that business is competitive and that winning is everything.

- **Self-starter**
The company values people who take the initiative to do what needs to be done. It values people who take action and don't wait for direction.

- **Risk taker**
The company values people who aren't afraid to take risks. It values people who understand that the greatest gains are those that come from tak-

ing the greatest risks but understand that by taking a risk, they must make every effort to limit the company's exposure and liability.

- **Team player**

The company values people who understand the benefits of teamwork and have a deep desire to be part of a team. It values people who put the needs of the team ahead of their own and help teammates in need.

## PERSONALITY

To be considered for the position, the candidates must possess most of the personality traits enumerated below and deemed necessary for the candidates to be successful in this position:

- The candidates must work with persons in product marketing, marketing communications, quality assurance, and customer support. To that end, the candidates must be personable and work well with others. They should be interesting people to talk with and have a strong desire to build strong relationships.
- The candidates must have a high energy level. They must be people who will dig for the information that they need, and seek out and effectively utilize the persons who can provide them the information necessary to complete their job.
- The candidates must not be easily intimidated, but readily admit their technical weaknesses. They should be able to stand toe-to-toe with the leads on the various development projects.

## TRACK RECORD

To be considered for the position, candidates must have a history of having successfully applied their knowledge and skills to produce significant results:

- The ideal candidates must have a history of completing projects and have worked on "large" projects requiring coordination of effort among several people each focusing on a different aspect of the project.
- The candidates must be results oriented, not process oriented and should have faced difficulties or problems in the past similar to what they will experience here.

## KNOWLEDGE, SKILLS, AND EXPERIENCE

To be considered for the position, candidates must possess most of the knowledge and experience enumerated below and deemed necessary for the candidates to be successful in this position:

- The candidates must be people who will bring strong technical skills to the table, and will possess the ability to effectively translate those skills into an increase in productivity for the organization.
- Ideally, the candidates will have expertise in UNIX and C with knowledge of NT. They will have developed one or more projects in either C++ or Java outside an academic environment.
- The candidate should be comfortable with a command line interface and should readily see the value in scripting in their favorite shell or Perl.

## Hiring

### Finding candidates

It's getting more difficult to find qualified software development professionals these days. Finding the best of them is even harder. You'll have to use every source at your disposal. Let's look at a few.

#### Look within your own company

Who are the software developers in your organization who match the profile of the kind of person you're looking for? Are they approachable, i.e., can you recruit them?

#### Ask your employees

Your current employees are a great source for prospective new employees. People tend to refer people like themselves. If you find a person in your organization who matches the profile of the kind of person you're looking for but you can't hire them because they're not interested in your offer or they're committed to their current project, then ask them to refer someone.

#### Take advantage of the Internet

The Internet is another great source, but difficult to search due to the shear volume of resumes available from a variety of sources.

### Use agencies

I have a love-hate relationship with agencies. There are many agencies that have no idea how to properly qualify a candidate. And, there are some that do a fantastic job. The best advice I can give you is to try one. If they get the results you seek then keep using them; otherwise drop them and try another until you find one that gets good results.

### Professional societies

Most cities have local chapters of national societies of professionals who work in our industry. Some have regional societies that focus on issues unique to that area. They are great sources for prospective candidates.

### Use newspapers to draw in local talent

Yes, job seekers still use the newspaper! I've never been a big fan of using newspapers only because I've never found a job using one. However, I have had a number of good experiences drawing in local talent using the newspaper. On the up side, if you find a match, you don't have to pay the recruiter's fees. On the down side, you tend to get a large number of poor-fit resumes.

## Do they fit?

You've established a hiring profile and found candidates who appear to match your profile on paper. How do you determine whether they fit that profile?

### Prepare your questions ahead of time

Be prepared. Few interviewers are prepared for an interview. More often than not, they read a candidate's resume for the first time either shortly before or during the interview. Being prepared does two things: it helps you to accurately determine whether a candidate fits your profile, and it lets candidates know they are serious contenders for the position. Regarding the latter point, have you ever been interviewed by someone who was unprepared? I'm most certain that you have. How did that make you feel? Don't let your candidates feel that way.

### Their resume is your guide

It's easy for an interview to get off course. Spending too much time talking about yourself, overselling the company or position, and talking about things like hobbies, personal interests, and the like are common ways that interviews wander from their primary purpose. Remember, your objective is to determine whether the candidates fit your profile.

The best way to stay on course is to use their resume as your guide. Write your questions directly on it. Review your questions before the interview. Make sure they are sufficient in terms of breadth and depth. In other words, your questions must probe the four dimensions of the hiring profile to a depth that will allow you to accurately measure fit.

*Walking the talk*

Unlike interviewers, most job seekers prepare for an interview. Their agents, the recruiters, discover your hiring profile—often tailoring the candidate's resume to match it, or they sell you on how great a fit the candidate is regardless of whether they really are. Candidates will study subjects that appear on their resume that perhaps they don't know very well or with which they have little or no practical experience. A person's resume will paint the best possible picture of that person. You must peel back the onion to see what lies underneath.

Another useful metaphor that illustrates this point is to view interviewing like pulling on loose strands of yarn in a sweater. If after pulling on the first strand you end up with a short piece of yarn, find the next one and pull. If after pulling every loose strand you end up with a handful of short pieces, you likely have yourself a candidate who lacks depth.

### Red flags

*Long career at one company versus short careers at many companies*

There was a time when job hopping—staying at a job for less then five to 10 years—was considered bad. In our industry, finding someone who has stayed at a particular company for more than two years can sometimes be a challenge. But there are certainly many who do. And it is both a blessing and a curse. On the one hand, a person who has stayed with a company for many years has demonstrated the ability to commit long-term. On the other hand, all of his experience, i.e., his knowledge about how to develop software, markets, corporate culture, and the like are confined to one or a small number of perspectives. The person who has stayed with one large company for many years but has changed jobs internally, roughly every couple of years, may have a broader perspective on such things, but will still have much less exposure to variety than the person who changes companies every couple of years.

*The career contractor who wants to go permanent*

Career contractors who have decided they've had enough with contracting and wants a permanent job should be approached with extreme caution. Career contractors are people who have spent their entire careers moving from one 3-to-6 month project to another. Some do this for a decade or more. Most of the ones I've talked to say that the reason they went into contracting was the lure of varied assignments, travel to new and exotic places, like Detroit, being self-employed, and getting paid much better. Then, they say, after doing that for 10 or more years, they've grown tired of it all and want to settle down into something more permanent. They sound as if they want to retire!

Hiring people who want to settle down should be a warning sign to you. Aside from that, you can't build a team with transients. Teams take time to build, to get to know each other, figure out how to work with each other, optimize the way they work together, and so on. Approach the career contractors with extreme caution.

### Other tips

*Raise the collective IQ of your organization*

The idea of raising the collective IQ of your organization is an idea that I borrowed from a former colleague. I was discussing the hiring practices of my wife's company with him. Her company, an Austin-based software company, only hires people who demonstrate a high degree of intelligence during the interview process. How they do this is really quite simple: the interviewers only hire people they consider smarter than themselves. My colleague observed that each new hire pushes up the collective IQ of the organization. Over time, the organization grows smarter. A smart organization produces smart results.

*Hire someone you'd like to work for*

Another bit of hiring advice given to me by Bill Bock was that you should only hire people that you'd like to work for. The idea is not unlike that of raising the collective IQ of your organization. If you're good at what you do and hire someone who you think is better, over time the organization will grow more competent. A competent organization produces competent results.

*Trust your gut*

Interviewing experts say you should not hire someone based on a gut feeling. Although I agree with them if it's the only basis of a hiring decision, I don't agree with those who say you should ignore or diminish the importance of such a feeling. In particular, there are two gut feelings you should pay particular attention to: (1) something just doesn't seem right about this person, and (2) he's too good to be true.

*1. Something just doesn't seem right about this person*

Have you ever interviewed someone and felt that something just wasn't quite right? Worse, you can't explain why you feel that way? Don't ignore that feeling just because you can't explain it.

*2. He's too good to be true*

Then, there's the person who has always done everything right. You ask if he has any weakness and he says no. His resume seems to have been tailor-made for the position you're hiring for. You start wondering if this person is real. If you suspect that someone is too good to be true, he probably is. Be suspicious.

### Sell the opportunity

Before you can sell someone something, you must understand her needs and wants. Sound familiar? It's entirely possible, in fact, it happens quite often, that you'll find someone who is a strong fit with your profile but doesn't want the job. Typically, she doesn't want it because she perceives it to be a poor fit with her profile. In other words, she is interviewing you as much as you are interviewing her.

Before you begin to sell your company to the candidate and the position for which she is interviewing, determine her profile. It's as simple as asking the question, "What are you looking for?" As she responds, listen carefully. Don't try to map what she's saying to what you have to offer. Look for opportunities to probe deeper in the four areas of the hiring profile. In other words, she has needs and wants with respect to culture, personality, experience, and intellectual fulfillment.

After you understand the needs and wants, and only then, map the opportunity that you have to offer and present it to the candidate.

### Make them an offer they can't refuse

Assuming that the opportunity you have to offer is compelling to the candidate, the last hurdle to overcome is the financial side of the deal. You should know what the candidate is looking for before she ever sets foot in your door. If you are not prepared to exceed her expectations, don't bring her in. You will be setting yourself up for failure.

There are several things that can go wrong when you try to sell a candidate a financial package that is below her expectations. First, you insult her by effectively saying she is not worth what she is seeking, consequently, she will turn down the offer; you have to start the process all over again with another candidate. Another possible outcome is that you successfully convince her to accept something less than she wants. Later, after she's had time to reflect on the deal, she may realize that she's been duped. Of course, then she may resent you and you have a much bigger problem to deal with.

I'm not suggesting that you pay people whatever they want. You must determine what they want before they come in and make sure it fits your financial plan. If you make them an offer, don't haggle. If they're what you're looking for, offer something that is financially compelling. It will make closing the deal easier and avoid the more serious problem of employee resentment later on.

### Close the deal fast

In today's competitive market for technical talent, time is of the essence. If you've concluded that you want to hire someone, make the offer before the candidate leaves your office. If possible, get his acceptance before he leaves. If he must think about the offer, for example, to consult with his spouse or family, place a short fuse on the offer, create a sense of urgency. In other words, don't give the candidate a chance to shop around for a competitive offer.

## Organize Around Products

### Traditional Hierarchical Organizations

#### What is a traditional hierarchical organization?

##### *Divides organization into independent functional units*

Most companies group together people who share a common functional responsibility and then connect those functional groupings by a hierar-

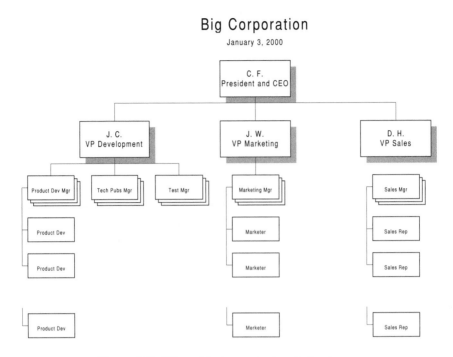

**Figure 2-3** Hierachical organizational structure

chical management structure. Communication between two functional units flows up from one unit to the level of management that they share in common and back down to the other. Tactical decisions are often made either by the group of managers representing all the functional units involved or by the manager they share in common up the hierarchy. A traditional hierarchical organization might look like the one depicted in Figure 2-3:

### Why they don't work

#### *Optimized for vertical communication and decision making*

There are two characteristics of such an organizational structure that undermine a team's ability to perform at its best. The first is that communication flows along the longest rather than the shortest path. The second is that tactical decision making, i.e., decisions related to the creation and execution of tactical plans, is made up of the hierarchy rather than by the team that must execute that plan.

To illustrate how such organizations work, consider this example. Imagine that you're a quality assurance engineer and you discover a problem while testing a product that you believe is severe enough that it must be fixed before the product is released to market. Since your company's organized in a traditional fashion, you report the problem to your manager, the manager of the quality assurance department. He listens carefully to your argument and chooses to support your crusade to halt the product based on your impassioned plea. He takes it to his boss, the director of product development.

Both your manager and his are busy people. It takes them a few days to get together to discuss the problem you've found and to debate what action to take. Finally, they get together to review the case. Your boss does a fine job repeating what you said, but because he's not as familiar with the details as you are, he's unable to answer some of the probing question that his boss asks. He has to go back to you for more information before his boss is willing to support your recommendation.

A few days later, with details in hand, your boss and his get together again. This time, his boss agrees that there is merit to your argument and asks his administrative assistant to arrange a meeting to include the manager of QA, the manager of engineering who manages the team implementing the product, and himself.

The meeting takes place a few days later. Once again, the case is reviewed. But, by now, much of the passion and conviction behind your plea is lost. During the discussion, broader business issues are discussed such as potential impact on quarterly revenue if the product is held up, press and analyst reaction to a delay, loss of market share to a competitor releasing a new version of their product ahead of yours, and the like. The problem that you discovered, a severe defect that any reasonable and rational person would conclude must be fixed, is hardly discussed.

In the end, the trio of managers concludes that the problem must be fixed. They pass the word back down both branches of the hierarchy that the defect you reported must be fixed. That doesn't sound particularly efficient does it? Is your organization like the one I just described? If so, change it or move to a new one.

## Flat Organizations

### What is a flat organization?

During the 1980s, a trend toward flat and wide organizational structures became popular primarily for two reasons: (1) to reduce the number of people involved in communicating information up and down the organization, and (2) middle management was seen as redundant.

### Why they don't work

The upside of this kind of organization is that there are indeed less people involved in communicating information up and down the organization. The down side is that senior management has less time to focus on the process of strategic business decision making as they get drawn in to address more tactical issues that were previously handled by the middle managers. And, when they shift their attention from more tactical business decision making to strategic, they tend to ignore the former often leaving the organization below them without leadership.

At first glance this may seem like a good thing. Doesn't it shift tactical decision making down to lower levels in the organization? Isn't that a good thing? Well, yes and no. As you'll see in the next section, it is a good thing if you've eliminated functional boundaries. But with functional boundaries in place, pushing down tactical decision making can be disastrous. Without tactical operational leadership, organizational efficiency deteriorates as the leaderless lower echelon of the organization wanders off in various directions.

## A Better Way

### Product development requires a cross-functional body of people

It's rare for a software developer working independently to develop a software product that turns into a commercial success, but it does happen. Those stories fuel the fantasies of thousands of aspiring entrepreneurs. Unfortunately, for every such success there are countless cases of failure that you never hear about.

The development of a commercially successful product requires the talents of numerous different professionals across many different functions. If they are only allowed to communicate through vertical channels it will take longer for the message to travel from its origin to its destination. As the message passes from one person in the chain up to the next and finally down the other side, it is likely to change; do you remember the telephone game you may have played as a child? Pushing tactical decision making higher up into the organization will attenuate the process of developing software making it much less efficient.

### Create a cross-functional team

The most effective teams, i.e., the ones that reach their objectives and are therefore high performance teams, are the ones that are organized around projects not functions and where tactical decision making, i.e., decisions related to execution of the plan, is pushed down to the team. In such an organization, communication and decision making is primarily horizontal with occasional vertical communication to keep upper levels of management informed and to occasionally draw on them to help get past tactical sticking points.

### Appoint a leader with cross-functional responsibility

In such an organization, the project team consists of everyone involved in the process of conceiving, implementing, and delivering a product to market. Leadership of such a team should be held by a single person from start to finish. Their background should include strong project management skills and experience, in-depth skill and experience in at least one if not two or three functional areas, and a mimimum basic knowledge of the others. They should be detail oriented and diplomatic—and have strong interpersonal skills. Such an organization might look like the one in Figure 2-4.

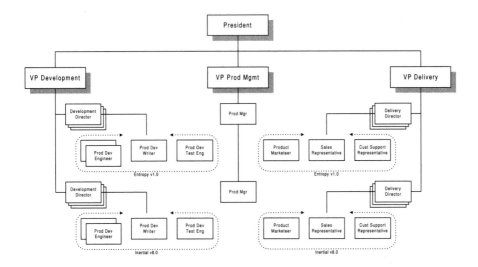

**Figure 2-4** Cross-functional team-oriented organizational structure

# CHAPTER 3

# Prepare the Team

## Eliminate Team Weaknesses

### Individual weaknesses versus team weaknesses

When you look at a team, you can look at it from two different perspectives. One is to look at the individuals on the team and the other is to view the team as a whole. Individuals operating independently exhibit certain characteristics and behaviors. When you bring that group of individuals together to work toward a common set of objectives, that group viewed as a single entity exhibits certain characteristics and behaviors different from any of the individuals on the team; this is sometimes referred to as the *group dynamic*. The other effect of bringing together a group of people to work toward common objectives is called synergy. Synergy is when the net result of a team exceeds what the individual team members can produce working independently. This is sometimes referred to as two heads are better than one or 1+1=3. Whether there is synergy and the degree to which it exists when present is a function of the group dynamic.

A positive group dynamic and maximum synergy sometimes happens naturally, but that's leaving it to chance. You can create such teams, and you must do it intentionally. It starts by hiring the best (recall Chapter 2). Once you've hired the best, and before you focus them on their objectives (Chapter

6), you must prepare them. The first step in preparing the team is to identify and eliminate team weaknesses.

### Focus on determining team weaknesses

Don't focus all of your time trying to fine tune individual team member performance. Focusing on individual performance is like giving a car a tune up by investing all your time changing its oil. Sure, new oil will help the car perform better, but what about new spark plugs? View the team as if it were an individual. Focus on eliminating shortcomings that undermine the team's ability to achieve maximum synergy.

Determining weaknesses is difficult because to do it properly requires you to forget everything you know about your own strengths and weaknesses. In other words, you have to look at the team in absolute terms rather than relative terms. Humans don't do that naturally. For example, if you're the leader of a team of software developers and you happen to have been a meticulous software developer at one time in your career you will tend to hire, admire, and promote other developers that share your style; this is sometimes referred to as the like-promotes-like phenomena. Consciously or subconsciously, you'll likely see everyone else as being weak in this area if they don't approach software development with the same care you did. Although it's rarely the case that you'd want the team to approach software development carelessly, there are circumstances where it is less important. For example, if you're leading a team responsible for creating hot fixes for a product, you may need software developers who are quick to resolve problems versus those who are extremely thorough. If that's what you need, that's what you've hired, and that's what they do, you can't say they are weak in that particular area.

## Eliminate Weaknesses by Harnessing Strengths

If you focus your attention on only the team's weaknesses, you will not fully take advantage of their strengths. Identify and exploit their strengths. For example, if a team ends up being good at maintaining software, don't assign that team a project to design and implement a new product from the ground up.

# Fill In the Holes in Their Skills and Experience

## Identify

Since you've hired people with appropriate knowledge, skills, and experience there should be few holes. But there will be some, and it is important to identify them and fill them in before starting the project. Filling in those holes means training, but training can serve other purposes as well. There are a number of excellent ways to gain the knowledge and basic skills you need to fill in a hole. I've found both book studies and formal training to be very effective.

### Book studies

The thing I like best about book studies is that they are easy to organize, convenient, and inexpensive. Book studies can be conducted a number of different ways. One way is to meet with the study group once or twice a week reviewing a chapter at a time. At each meeting ask a different member of the group to be responsible for leading the review of that chapter.

### Formal training

Formal training is another excellent way to fill in the holes. It is available in many forms, from computer based training, seminars, and lectures to graduate school certificates and degree programs. One form of formal training that has been gaining in popularity is interactive Web-based training. By using video and audio conferencing commonly available in Web browsers and plug-in technologies, more and more people are taking courses, indeed, getting their degrees, over the Internet. The virtual campus has arrived and it is here to stay.

# CHAPTER 4

# Prepare to Lead

## People Are People Not Resources

A mistake commonly made by both inexperienced and experienced managers is to forget that they lead people. What are people? That seems like a silly question to ask, doesn't it? But, how often have you thought about what it means to be a person? How would you describe human beings to an alien? Among other things, you might say that humans are capable of experiencing and expressing a broad range of emotions. They can love and hate, be generous or stingy, be giving or selfish, be concerned about the welfare of others or self-centered. They can be law abiding or criminal. Childhood experiences shape their adult behavior. Adult experiences affect how they behave later in life. Good people turn bad. Bad people turn good. Some people have deep-seated behaviors that cannot be changed or would require tremendous effort to change through years of intensive therapy.

The bottom line is that people are complex—far beyond the most complex machines ever devised. Treat them as if they were simple machines, like computers for example, and you will most certainly regret having made such an assumption.

## People Have Needs, Resources Need Maintenance

### People

Equally important to fulfilling the needs of your customers is fulfilling the needs of your employees. After all, your employees make it possible for you to fulfill your customers' needs. Why should their needs be any less important? Fulfilling those needs keeps your employees interested and coming back for more. Each employee will have unique needs, but all tend to have some in common. These include having meaningful work to perform, being part of a team, being fairly compensated for their work, and having confidence they are working toward something specific and of significance.

#### *Meaningful work*

The definition of meaningful work depends on one's personal preferences. There are software developers who find debugging difficult customer problems deeply satisfying and meaningful, while others find it painfully unfulfilling. Others prefer to refine an existing product through innovation to strengthen its position against a competitor, to broaden its appeal, or to push the product into a new or related market. Still others prefer to invent something new. What is true for each of them is that they want to spend the majority of their time performing what they consider meaningful work. Ask software architects to fix bugs for six months and they'll probably quit. Ask people who have spent their careers as ustomer problem troubleshooters to spend 18 months designing and implementing a single product, i.e., solving a single problem over an 18 month period, and sooner or later they'll quit too!

Find out what each member of your team finds meaningful and do your best to match their needs with your project objectives. If you cannot, be honest with yourself and them. Work together to create a win-win transition onto something they will find rewarding.

#### *Part of a team*

For those outside the software industry, software developers are often thought of as introverted nerds, loners who keep to themselves and spend all day (and all night) thinking about and playing with their computers. They are considered social misfits who prefer to hide in dark offices and would rather interact with others electronically than in person. There are certainly people in our industry who fit that description, but they are in the minority.

Most software development professionals are social people and prefer a high degree of interaction with their peers and leaders. They derive great comfort from knowing that others are engaged in their struggle to develop a new product or repair an aging one. They thrive when they are part of a team and lead by competent leaders and flounder when working alone or without leadership. They prefer to be part of a team.

### Fair compensation

Who likes to get paid less than they are worth? Nobody. Software developers, like everyone else, want to be compensated fairly for their knowledge, skills, experience, and the results they produce. But fair is relative. Your challenge as their leader is to determine what fair means to each of them. To one software developer, it might mean being paid as well as their peers. To others, it might mean being paid as well as their counterparts at other companies. And, of course, nobody minds being paid too much.

### A destination and a course

Imagine getting on an airplane believing it is destined for Palo Alto, California, and hearing an announcement from the captain that you are about to embark, destination: nowhere in particular. Wait a second, "What happened to Palo Alto?" you ask the flight attendant. "The flight engineer doesn't feel like plotting a course to Palo Alto so the captain has decided to fly us around for a while. We'll land somewhere just before we run out of fuel!" replies the flight attendant.

Seems absurd doesn't it? Sadly, this happens frequently in our business. We bring people on board promising to take them somewhere specific and end up flying around sightseeing until we run out of fuel and crash. People want to know where you are taking them and then they look for signs that you are on course. If they sense that you have misled them, or are flying off course and just sightseeing, they'll bail out. These days, where the demand for software development professionals far exceeds the supply, they all are wearing parachutes, standing in the doorway ready to jump.

### Praise

Praise comes in many forms. There's the unexpected gift certificate given to the software developer who went the extra mile to finish an important project task. Or, public recognition at a company meeting acknowledging the outstanding accomplishments of a project team. There's the private thank you to the aspiring team lead who helped two of his teammates resolve a difference of opinion. Some people prefer to be praised in private, others like public recognition. Regardless, most everyone likes to be praised.

To be effective, praise must be sincere. If you consciously use it as a tool, you're likely to come across as insincere. Instead, develop the habit of spontaneous sincerity, i.e., heartfelt praise. Express your emotions? I bet you thought you had to be stoic to be an effective leader. Not true. Some of the most effective leaders I have ever met come across as real people not facsimiles of George S. Patton.

### Resources

Do resources have needs? I'm not sure. The last time I asked my computer what it needed it didn't reply. If one of its components, such as the disk drive, were to fail, I could easily replace it. And, of course, there are a variety of preventive maintenance tasks I could perform to prevent failures and to maintain a high degree of usability; for example, cleaning fingerprints off the screen, blowing crumbs out of the keyboard, vacuuming dust out off the motherboard, and so on. If they break, you fix or replace them. If they're too slow, you upgrade them.

But repairing broken components and performing preventive maintenance is not the same as satisfying a human need. Resources, like computers, don't really *need* anything. Resources don't need to perform meaningful work, they don't need to be part of a team, they don't require compensation, a destination, or a course to follow, and they certainly don't need to be praised. Well, it might not hurt to praise them once in awhile.

## People Learn, Resources Are Programmed

### People

What does it mean to learn how to do something new? It means more than simply acquiring new knowledge. Learning involves developing a feel for what you are doing. It comes after you've applied that knowledge enough times to develop a sense that you are doing it right. Developing a feel for something or a sense that you are doing something right is clearly a human capability that we don't share with the machine.

#### *Acquiring knowledge*

#### *Read*

Reading a book or an article is an inexpensive way to acquire new knowledge. Inexpensive? You might be thinking that this book cost you a small fortune! I used to think like that too, but realized after writing my first book that the value of the information contained in it was enormous. I captured and conveyed more than a decade's worth of experience that you can leverage for the mere cost of a new pair of denim pants. Of course, the author of every book thinks they know the best way to do something.

As a leader, recommend books to your teammates that you've read and found helpful in developing your knowledgebase. Copy articles you've read and distribute them (after getting permission from the copyright owner). Conduct book studies (see Chapter 3).

*Listen*

Listening to others speak on a topic that you'd like to learn more about is another excellent way to acquire knowledge. Formal classes at the local university, Web seminars, conferences, and the like are all easy and effective ways to pick up new information.

As a leader, you should put together and conduct presentations of interest and importance on subjects for which you've developed that feeling I referred to earlier. For example, if you find that your team lacks the basic knowledge to properly plan a project, put together a how-to presentation on the subject. Then, help them develop their planning skills. Remember not to assume that because you provided them with knowledge, they've developed the skill that follows the application of that knowledge. Follow your training session with coaching to help them plan their next project. Provide assistance as they execute that plan. Give them room to experiment and make mistakes. Give them enough room to learn but not so much that they fail.

*Copy*

Another way to acquire knowledge is to watch and copy someone who has already acquired the knowledge and skill that you wish to possess. In other words, find a role model. If, for example, you'd like to learn more about giving an effective presentation, find someone who's considered an effective presenter, watch them present, and then give a presentation of your own patterning it after their style.

As a leader, it is important to remember that others are learning from you by studying and copying you. In particular, your subordinates are watching you closely whether you realize it or not. If you want them to learn the right way, and you do, then always set the right example. You must walk the talk. Your peers and superiors are also watching and learning from you.

One way to determine whether others see you as a leader in some area is to recognize when they are copying you. Have you ever been in a situation where you suddenly realized that someone is using certain gestures or mannerisms that you use? Or, they are repeating what you said to them to someone else as if it were their idea? Perhaps you've noticed someone handling a particular situation in the same way that you handled a similar situation? All of these are signs that you are being copied. Remember that old saying: "Imitation is the sincerest form of flattery."

### *Learning*

When you've learned how to do something, you've developed a feel for doing it properly. To say you have learned something means you have mastered or you are skilled at that thing. Skill is developed over time and comes through repetition. It also helps if you have a coach or mentor who can watch you apply your knowledge and help guide you as you become skilled. Having a coach or mentor, though, isn't always a blessing. The most effective way to develop the feeling that you are doing something right is to feel what it is like to do it wrong.

#### *Lessons from flying*

One of the first things you are taught while learning how to fly airplanes is how to take off and land. First, you read a book to learn the steps. Then, you watch a video tape that shows an experienced pilot flawlessly performing the steps. Next is the lecture from your ground school instructor who repeats the information one more time. Finally, you get to fly the plane. In the plane, your flight instructor repeats the information again, shows you how to perform the steps by example, and then lets you try.

A number of years ago, I thought I'd give flying a try. My first attempts to take off and land the plane went without incident. But that presented a problem. My instructor wanted me to make a particular landing mistake so she could show me how to recover. It was one of the lessons I had to learn prior to soloing. Let me explain.

On final approach, in a Cessna 172, you are flying at a fixed speed, 60 knots, flaps down, nose aimed at the numbers on the end of the runway. Once you reach a point just above the runway, you begin to slowly pull back on the yoke to raise the nose. This is called flaring. The effect is that the plane begins to slow down and settle to the ground. As you lose speed, though, you also lose lift which causes the nose to drop. To keep the nose up, so that you land on the main gear first, you have to slowly and continuously pull back the yoke until the main gear makes contact with the runway. If you pull the yoke back too far, you eventually slow down to the wing's stall speed, the nose will abruptly drop, and you'll auger into the runway. If you don't pull the yoke back at all, holding it steady after the flare, you'll lose lift and stall. When that happens, the nose gear touches down first, then the main gear touches down forcefully causing the nose to bounce up in the air. You then begin to undulate like a porpoise down the runway until you finally drive the nose and propeller into the ground and flip the plane over! Clearly, this is not a good thing. But, there is a procedure to recover from such a situation.

On my next landing, my instructor caused the plane to porpoise by holding the yoke steady after the flare and then demonstrated the recovery procedure. I then practiced the recovery procedure a few times.

A few weeks later, my instructor decided that it was time for me to solo. It was a strange feeling not having someone next to me in the right seat to bail me out if I made a mistake. My first take off went smoothly. I stayed in the pattern and came around to land. Everything was going by the book, up until the flare. I flared the plane; everything seemed to be going fine. Next thing I knew I was bouncing down the runway like a porpoise. Yikes, that was unnerving! I executed the recovery procedure and went around the pattern for another attempt. It happened again. I recovered. By now, however, I was quite nervous. I wasn't sure why this was happening.

My instructor's voice came over the radio asking me if everything was OK. I told her I was fine, but not sure what I was doing wrong. She told me to keep calm and try again. What choice did I have, I thought? I had to land the plane. I couldn't just pull over and get out. Then, it dawned on me. The reason I was bouncing down the runway was that I wasn't slowly pulling back the yoke after the flare to keep the nose up. On my next attempt, I landed the plane.

That experience was key for me to understand the lesson my instructor was trying to teach me. Although she taught me how to do it, it wasn't until I tried it on my own and made a few mistakes attempting to apply that knowledge that I truly understood. I developed a feeling that allowed me to recognize when things were going right and when they were going wrong. And, when they went wrong, I knew what to do make it right.

### Resources

Of course, resources don't read books nor do they attend lectures to acquire new knowledge about how to perform a new task. They don't apply that knowledge to learn. In fact, they can't really *learn* anything. Remember, learning involves developing a feeling that you're doing something right. With that feeling, you're able to recognize when something is going wrong.

## People Quit, Resources Break

### People

Most people shy away from the things that cause them pain and toward the things that give them pleasure. Unfulfilled needs are painful. Given a choice between a job that will satisfy their needs and one that will not, most people will choose the former. If the former is with another company, they'll quit and go to work for that other company. In some cases, that may be a good thing. But, there are much more effective ways to transition an employee whose needs you cannot fulfill out of your organization and into one that is a better fit for them. I cover that subject in Chapter 6.

### Resources

As mentioned earlier, resources don't have needs per se. They'll do anything you ask them to do, assuming they have the capacity to do so. And, they'll keep doing it over and over again without complaint until they break. When they break, you can throw them out or fix them. Once replaced or fixed, they'll return to performing the task that they've been programmed to perform—again, without complaint.

## You Must Be a Leader Before You Can Lead

### I'm a Manager, Doesn't That Make Me a Leader?

### Classic distinction between manager and leader

The term "manager" is often defined using words such as plans, directs, organizes, and controls which describe the manager's responsibilities. On the other hand, the term "leader" is typically defined in terms of attributes that people possess who are generally recognized as leaders. For example, leaders are viewed as people who are confident, decisive, knowledgeable, and intelligent, and treat people with respect and fairness.

### Management is assigned, leadership is earned

When you become a manager, you are granted the authority to commit to and direct the company's resources toward the fulfillment of its vision. This authority is granted to you by a superior manager or, if you're the top manager, i.e., the CEO, by the board of directors. Having such authority, however, does not make you a leader.

Leaders, on the other hand, have mastered the art of influence. They rarely ever need to invoke their authority to direct their team to achieve their objectives. One way to distinguish managers from leaders is to characterize them as either pushing their team toward their objectives, like a cattleman would drive a herd back to the corral, or pulling their team toward their objectives by standing out in front of them and showing them the way. Managers push and leaders pull.

## Is It Possible to Be Effective If You Are Not a Leader?

### What does it mean to be effective?

A leader's effectiveness is measured by examining his team's achievements over time. It is easy to recognize the leader of a high performance software development team as the one leading the team that consistently achieves or exceeds its objectives.

### Leadership is a prerequisite for effectiveness

Leaders pull their teams toward their objectives. But people won't follow just anyone, unless forced. When forced, they will not perform to their greatest potential. They often don't get the job done and when they do, they typically have missed major objectives along the way. To be effective, you must lead. If you cannot, get out of the way and let someone else lead.

### Do others see you as a manager or a leader?

The good news is that if after determining whether you are a manager or a leader, you have concluded that you are a manager, you can become a leader. It won't be easy but it can be done. The best way to make such a change is to understand what leaders look like and then to emulate them. As you work to become one, you must measure whether you're making the transformation successfully and then make adjustments as needed.

If, on the other hand, you've concluded that you are a leader then you must test your assertion. You will undoubtedly find that although you may be perceived as a leader there is room for improvement. Many studies have been done to determine what makes a leader a leader. All conclude that leaders consistently possess an abundance of certain qualities that can be placed into one of three categories: conduct, style, and skill. How many of the following apply to you?

Attributes of a successful leader:
- Conduct
  - Projects air of confidence
  - Effortlessly handles difficult situations
  - Behaves consistently and predictably
  - Self-directed, often taking the initiative
  - Timely decision maker
- Style
  - Provides encouragement
  - Enthusiastic
  - Places team ahead of self
  - Loyal to the team
  - Treats people with respect
  - Fair
- Skill
  - Knowledgeable
  - Solves problems quickly and creatively
  - Consistently demonstrates sound judgment

### Perception is everything

***What is your perception?***

Based on your answer to the question posed above, what is your perception about your own leadership abilities?

***Do others perceive you as a leader?***

It's a little tricky to figure this one out, but not impossible. I suggest that you go to members of your staff, peers, or your superiors and ask them if they think you're a leader. If the consensus is yes, then keep doing what you're doing. Otherwise, identify areas for improvement (use the attributes above as a guide), develop an improvement plan for yourself, and execute it.

## Trickle-Down Effect of Leadership

Have you ever heard the expression, "Lead by example"? The assumption inherent in this expression is that the example you lead by is a good one. Every person in a position of leadership leads by example whether they want to or not. Whether they appear to be, your subordinates are always watching you and examining, recording, and copying your behavior. Consequently, you must be self-aware to ensure that the behaviors you want them to copy are the ones you exhibit. The others must be checked. This is the trickle-down effect of leadership.

## Barriers to Effective Leadership

Many things can interfere with both the practice and cultivation of leadership. Certain cultural traits, beliefs, and behaviors can, if present, undermine a leader's effectiveness and discourage those with strong tendencies toward leadership from rising up within the organization. If you are the CEO or in a position to effect changes in your culture and the composition of your team, my advice to you is to do everything in your power to eliminate anti-leadership barriers in your organization. Let's take a look at some of the most insidious of these barriers.

### Popularity Contests

There is a difference between being well liked as a manager and being popular. To be popular, one must make popular decisions. These aren't always the right decisions. Leadership is about making the right decisions. If you would rather be popular, then step out of the way and let someone else lead.

### Politics

What are politics? People making backroom deals. Exchanging favors. Working their way into the in crowd. Distancing themselves from the out crowd. Spreading rumors. Back stabbing. Being transparent.

How do politics act as a barrier to leadership? They defocus the team. When the team is not focused, they miss achieving their objectives. How do you eliminate this barrier? You can't because such behaviors are an inherent part of being human. It is hard to resist being human. I'll wager that these behaviors are coded into our genes and that we will always be this way. Sounds hopeless, doesn't it? It's not. But all you can do is focus on containing it. How? Easy. Identify those that focus an inordinate amount of their time and energy practicing such behaviors. Expose them, i.e., call them on their behavior. Tell them to stop engaging in such behavior immediately. If they don't, fire them.

### Bureaucracy

Bureaucrats are people who spend all of their time creating and following processes for the sake of creating and following processes. They are easy to spot; they want to solve every problem by creating a new process. Once created, they rarely ever change them and will blindly follow a process until the end of time.

Hopefully, the barrier to leadership is obvious; engaging in activities that provide little if any help in getting you to your objectives, but, instead, lead you away, should be eliminated.

## Prepare to Lead

### Identify Your Weaknesses

You must learn how to identify your own weaknesses and do everything you can to eliminate them. If you don't, someone else will. That person might be a competitor, or a colleague vying for your position, or a peer or subordinate seeking to undermine your efforts. It is not easy to identify your own weaknesses. You will need help.

## Eliminate Your Weaknesses

### Find a mentor and a coach

I cannot overemphasize the importance of having a good mentor and a good coach. Both can help you see things that you otherwise might miss. They can help point you in the right direction when you are lost and can guide you through difficult terrain. Your mentor should be someone who can help you develop into what you'd like to be in the future. Your coach should be someone who can help you improve your performance in your present job.

Both your mentor and coach should be carefully chosen. Imagine that you are about to climb Mount Everest. How much time would you spend selecting your guide? You'd probably want the best guide you could find. Pick your mentor and coach with the same scrutiny and care.

#### *Attributes of good mentors and coaches*

Good mentors and coaches share some attributes. Below, is a list of things to look for.

#### *Track record of success*

Hopefully this is obvious, but I felt compelled to point it out because there are plenty of people out there who are willing and eager to assume one or both roles but aren't qualified. In my opinion, the only people truly qualified to give advice about something are people who have a track record of success doing whatever it is they are giving advice on.

#### *Good listener*

Good listeners are hard to find. A good listener is someone who is completely engaged in the act of listening. They aren't thinking about what they are going to say when you are finished. They aren't building a rebuttal or challenge in their heads to something you said. They don't try to apply what they are hearing to their own personal experiences and perspective.

They are, however, listening to what you are saying and trying to understand it from your perspective. They follow listening with a moment of reflection, analysis, and action. Good mentors and coaches need to understand what you say from your perspective, look ahead to where you want to go, then help you build a path to get there. If they're not really listening to you or they map what you say back to their own personal experiences and perspective, they'll send you down a path that might be appropriate for them but not necessarily for you.

*Patient*

It takes a great deal of patience to be a mentor or a coach. As you walk the path toward your destination you'll have many questions, you'll make mistakes, and you'll stumble and will need help getting back on track. A person with little patience will be unable to provide you the time and attention required to do an effective job as your mentor or coach.

### *Where can you find one?*

*Not necessarily a superior*

Believe it or not, the guy (or gal) in charge didn't necessarily get promoted because they were the best at what they do. If you've been in the industry for any length of time, you've undoubtedly experienced first hand what it is like to work for someone less capable than you. Or worse, someone lacking even the most basic knowledge and skills needed to manage a team of software developers. I once worked for a company where all the product development managers were non-technical ex-marketers.

*Not necessarily at your company*

Don't constrain your search for a mentor and a coach to your company. Don't confine it to the same geography. In fact, the universe of prospective mentors and coaches spans our industry and beyond. Look to professionals in other industries.

When you start the search, plan to look far and wide. Use the Web to search for candidates. Once you've found one, get their e-mail address and send them a message. Tell them something about yourself and then ask if they're interested in being a mentor or a coach. If they are interested but are too far away to meet face-to-face, you can have a successful relationship via e-mail or phone.

*Professional societies*

Professional groups or associations are another excellent source to search for a mentor and a coach. Such societies are dedicated to bringing together people who share common professional backgrounds and interests. Many are membership-based and also open to anyone who's interested in attending lectures or seminars and the like. They typically have special interest groups that focus on a particular subject that is of interest only to a subset of the membership. Many have peer groups where participation is restricted to those who hold some particular place in a company's hierarchy—for example, a CEO peer group, or a vice president of engineering peer group.

### Referrals

Another way to search for a mentor and a coach is by referral. Ask your peers, your manager, friends, and associates at other companies.

### Fill in the holes in your skills and experience

### Lessons from a SCUBA diving vacation

About 10 years ago, I went on a SCUBA diving trip with a group of friends to Cozumel, Mexico. The diving was fantastic. This story is not about diving, though. The day before we left, we decided to take a trip to see the Mayan ruins on the island. To get there, we had to drive our rental car down a road full of potholes and I was driving. On the way in to see the ruins, I proceeded slowly, carefully avoiding the potholes. But on the way out, I grew impatient with our snail's pace and decided to drive through the potholes; after all I was driving a rental. Then, disaster hit. We struck a deep pothole and the battery in the rental flew from its mount and smashed the distributor cap and rotor. We had to hitchhike back to the hotel. Moral: don't ignore the holes. Figure out how to get around them or stop and fill them in.

Well, that's not the whole story. As we were driving out, before fate caught up with us, we passed a carload of people who were making their way out as cautiously as we had made our way in. My friend, sitting in the back and cocksure, smirked at the people in the other car as we passed them and yelled out, "This is the only way to travel!" and then laughed at them. A bit later, and further down the road where we had broken down, that carload of people my friend had just moments before insulted came inching toward us. Of course, by that time, we were stranded and needed help, at least to get back to our hotel. As they got closer, we started to wave them down for assistance. To our chagrin, they drove right by us. As they passed, a young girl in the passenger seat looked at us and said, "No, this is the only way to travel!" and they all laughed at us as they drove on. There are three morals to this story: (1) never assume that the shortest distance between two points is the fastest, (2) don't always bet on the hare (the turtle often wins), and (3) don't insult people whose help you might need someday.

### Fill in the holes

#### Read a book or two

It never ceases to amaze me when I hear someone say that they don't put much stock in what they read in professional books. Or, they've read a book or two and have concluded it was all hogwash so they've decided never to seek advice or counsel from such books. Clearly, some books are better than others, but most have at least a nugget or two that you can use to fill in a hole in your own knowledgebase. Has reading this book filled any of yours?

#### Attend formal training

You can benefit as much from formal training as the rest of your team. Set a good example and take classes with your team as well as others that may only be appropriate for you to take given your role. Let your team know that you're taking training. As I mentioned in Chapter 3, formal training comes in many forms, from interactive Web-based training and computer-based training to seminars, lectures, and graduate school certificate and degree programs.

# CHAPTER 5

# Planning

## By the Seat of Your Pants

Seat-of-your-pants projects can be exciting, but more often than not, they produce inferior results, and lead to team member burn out and attrition. There is no valid reason to manage a project this way. Project planning is a time-consuming and challenging activity yet absolutely necessary for high performance.

## Planning Is a Prerequisite for High Performance

Once again, you may recall from the Introduction that the definition of high performance used in this book is meeting or exceeding *all* of the objectives of a software development project. The purpose of a project plan is to map a course from where you are today to the set of objectives you've defined for a project. It does not provide the solution. The solution is what you get after you've successfully executed your plan.

Charting the course is the easy part. Navigating it is the tricky part. It's not like a leisurely drive through a familiar countryside where you have no particular destination in mind and time is unimportant. It's more like driving through the congested streets of a city that you've never been to before looking for an office building where you have an important meeting. With time running out, you find the building but can't find a parking spot. With just minutes to spare you find a parking spot and manage to make it up to the office just prior to the start of the meeting only to discover that you've left your presentation in the car.

All projects start with good intentions, but good intentions alone do not help you when you inevitably face challenges on your journey. Some challenges are minor. Others make scaling Mount Everest seem easy. Those challenges are the things that will put the success of your projects at risk.

A good project plan is the end result of a thorough analysis of a problem to be solved. It identifies the foreseeable challenges and offers alternate courses of action should they arise. Its purpose is to guide the effort from its starting point to its destination.

## There Is No Substitute for a Good Plan

Software development projects should be defined in terms of a problem to be solved regardless of the origin of the problem, i.e., customer need, market expansion, competitive threat, innovation, and so on. The problem statement is translated into a list of objective requirements.

Because project planning is imprecise, no matter how hard you try to develop the perfect plan you never will, so don't waste your time. The best you can hope for is that you've sufficiently mitigated risk. You cannot eliminate it nor can you avoid it. The worst plans fail to adequately mitigate risk or ignore it entirely. Typically, such plans read like prophecies. The requirements may be expressed in terms of objectives and the tasks may be well defined but dependencies are missing; challenges, if identified at all, are trite, and strategies for dealing with them omitted.

Successful projects, i.e., ones that reach their objectives, have project plans that mitigate risk by focusing the team on those objectives, letting others outside the team know what they're doing, acting as a tool that can be used to manage dependencies, and anticipating the challenges the team may face while executing the plan by offering alternate courses of action should they arise.

### Focuses Team

The best plans focus the team by defining a set of tasks that directly map back to the objectives of the project.

### Informs Others

In most organizations, development teams are responsible for developing the code. That leaves formal test and quality assurance, the creation of documentation, development of training materials, training of field personnel, and so on, to others. They need to know what you are doing in order for them to create and execute their plans. The best plans provide information that they need to be successful.

### Identifies Dependencies

All software projects have dependencies. These range from simple ones such as hardware and software, e.g., Microsoft Windows NT 4.0 SP4 running on an Intel 400 MHz processor with 64 MB of RAM, to complex ones like the completion of other projects or the hiring of developers with certain skills and experience. The best plans clearly identify project dependencies flagging those that may present unusual or extraordinary challenges.

### Anticipates Challenges and Offers Alternative Courses of Action

Challenges take many forms. One class of challenges was identified above—the challenge of satisfying all dependencies. Other kinds of challenges include staff turnover, new competitive threats, and customer satisfaction issues. Challenges put your project at risk of failing to achieve its objectives. They cannot be avoided. The best plans identify the challenges most likely to occur and offer ways to avoid or eliminate them.

## Project Planning Is Not an Exact Science

Project planning is imprecise for three main reasons: (1) you cannot break down a complex software project into all of its tasks and subtasks with absolute accuracy, (2) the people you will count on to execute those tasks are inherently unpredictable, and (3) unforeseen events will occur that will knock you off course.

### Task Breakdown Errors

The course is charted by laying out the individual steps you must follow to reach the objectives. In other words, it lists all of the things you must do to solve the problem. In effect, the problem is broken down into a series of subproblems each called a task. It's not until you execute one of these tasks, i.e., solve one of these subproblems, that you discover all of the detail associated with that task. You inevitably discover things that you could only uncover during execution, leading to the creation of new tasks and deletion or refinement of others.

### People Are Unpredictable

A project plan does more than lay out a list of tasks to be performed. It also identifies the people who will execute those tasks. The simplest project will depend on just one person; complex projects will depend on more. One reason that project planning is imprecise is that you cannot predict with certainty how well or how poorly each individual will execute their respective tasks. In fact, you can't predict with certainty whether they will complete the task at all. Throw in complex tasks that require groups of people to execute and task dependencies that need people to work in a coordinated fashion and suddenly you have a complex system of people that's even less predictable.

### Unforeseen Events

Not all challenges and alternatives can be identified ahead of time. There is no way to anticipate everything that might happen. If you try to, you will end up in an endless cycle of planning. Many projects fail simply because they never start. When unforeseen challenges appear, you must respond quickly and decisively. Many projects fail at this point because the project leader either fails to recognize a challenge or recognizes it but fails to respond quickly and decisively. Projects succeed more often than not when progress is measured against the plan and when quick and decisive actions are taken to counter any challenges, in particular the unforeseen challenges, that arise.

## Aim for 80% Accuracy in First Version of a Project Plan

### Don't guess

If you've been in the business of software development for any length of time, you are undoubtedly familiar with the time-honored tradition of guessing. This scene is all too common: someone from marketing or perhaps your manager walks by your office and asks, "So, Frank, how long do you think it would take you to whip up that shiny new feature we were talking about earlier?" To which you respond, "Gosh, Bill, I don't know, a couple of weeks." Next thing you know, the feature ends up in your company's marketing literature. Worse, the delivery of the new feature is listed in a sales agreement as a condition of the sale with a commitment to deliver it by the end of the quarter.

Over the course of my career, I am fortunate to have worked with some of the finest software developers in the world. The developers that I work with at BroadJump are without a doubt the finest of them all. But even they aren't good at guessing. When you guess, you are skipping the most important parts of the planning process, analysis and design. The result is an estimate that you cannot count on. Some software developers are better at this sort of estimating (or guesstimating) than others. Typically, they are seasoned veterans who are intimately familiar with the problem space, architecture, and implementation of the company's product line. Even then, however, their estimates aren't always dependable.

## Develop the Plan

In this section, you'll learn the planning process I use to plan my projects.

### Step 1—Put a stake in the ground

Producing a software product is much more than analysis, design, code, and test. I chose the word "produce" rather than "develop" to differentiate between the activity of creating the raw product, i.e., developing the product, and developing the product plus preparing it for sale, i.e., producing the product. Outside of developing the raw product, product data sheets must be created, training materials must be produced, and the sales and support organizations must be trained in preparation to sell and support the product. In most companies these tasks are performed by organizations outside of product development. Viewed as a Gantt chart, a typical project might look like the one in Figure 5-1.

It should be obvious that if Task 3 slips, then the downstream tasks will slip as well. In other words, implementation of the product is on the critical path (there's more about critical paths in an upcoming section). That leaves the downstream organizations waiting to start their tasks. When you consider

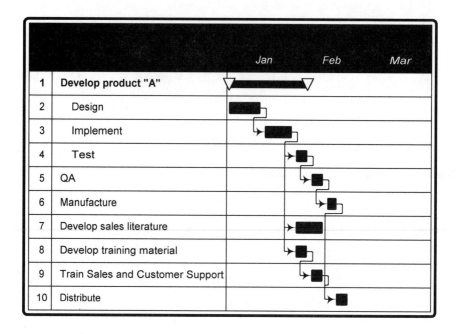

**Figure 5-1**   Typical software development project including production-related tasks.

the fact that most companies have more than one product development effort underway that shares the services of the downstream organizations, a slip in one project's product development phase can have a profound impact on the entire product delivery schedule. Viewed as a Gantt chart, such a project would look like the one in Figure 5-2.

An implicit objective of every project should be to prevent this effect from occurring. To do this, put a stake in the ground. This means you are going to commit to completing the development phase of the project by a certain date and that barring natural disasters and other events well outside your span of control, you will make that date. Of course, that date must be inside the window of opportunity identified in the product requirements (see Example 1-1). If after following all of the steps ahead you discover that the date is too aggressive, i.e., it falls outside of the window of opportunity, trim the requirements, or add more people to the team (if that will help), or both. You might even cancel the project! More on this process later.

One thing that is well within your span of control as the project's leader, is the quality of the plan that you develop. The only way you can con-

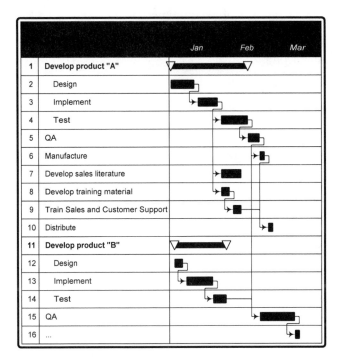

**Figure 5-2**  Effect of a software project slip on other projects contending for shared production-related services.

sistently make the date is by developing and following an accurate plan. The remaining sections of this chapter cover the planning step while Chapter 6 covers execution.

## Step 2—Specify the objectives

### *For each requirement, define a set of objectives*

From Chapter 1, you may recall that product requirements specify a solution to a problem. The requirements are specified in the form of specific features and functions, capabilities, performance metrics, and so on. Some are general, while others are very specific.

Objectives take the individual requirements in the product requirements document from the general to the specific (where the requirement is stated as a objective, it can be carried over directly from the requirements). For example, a general requirement such as:

"The product must meet or exceed the performance of the current release" is made specific by restating the requirement as a set of objectives:

"The product must encrypt a minimum of 1,000,000 characters per second using a 128-bit encoding scheme"

"The product must decrypt a minimum of 1,000,000 characters per second encoded using a 128-bit encoding scheme"

On the other hand, a specific requirement like:

"The product must decode documents encoded using the binhex64 encoding algorithm"

can be carried over directly as an objective.

### Step 3—For each set of related objectives, specify functional/design options

At this point, associated with each requirement is a set of one or more related objectives. Apply each step below to this set to create a set of functional/design option pairs. The relationship between requirements, objectives, and functional/design options is depicted in Figure 5-3.

### Step 3.1—Specify functional options, i.e., user visible effects of implementation

To satisfy a particular objective, it may be necessary to develop a user-visible feature. When possible, specify more than one way to satisfy that objective; however, there will be cases where it is necessary to restrict the way user-visible features look or behave. For example, the objective may be derived from a requirement that specifies the way a particular GUI dialog must look. When user-visible effects are not required to satisfy an objective, skip to the next step.

### Step 3.2—Specify high level design options, e.g., data flow diagrams, class diagrams, algorithms, and so on for each functional option

To achieve 80% confidence in your plan, an in-depth design is not necessary. Besides, why spend time developing detailed designs for a number of options that you'll ultimately toss out? What is necessary, however, is the development of a high-level design or, better stated, a design approach. It's needed because without it you cannot accurately assess the impact of each option, identify dependencies an option might have, determine how to test each option once implemented, and create a time estimate to complete the

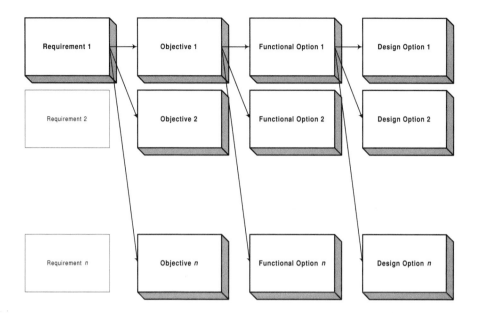

**Figure 5-3** Relationship between requirements, objectives, and functional/design options.

design, implement, and test of a particular option. In other words, your recommendation would be based purely on guesswork and gut feeling.

*Step 3.3—Identify impact of each functional/design option pair, e.g., impact on existing architecture, documentation, and so on.*

For some options, the impact on architecture, familiar behavior, documentation, and training materials may be low or none. For others, it may be profound. This step in the process of developing the plan is particularly important for the case where the impact is profound.

Imagine for a moment that you skip this step and guess incorrectly that a particular option will have little or no effect on anything outside of the code being written. Later, deep into the implementation, you discover that the option you've selected will make the next version of the product incompatible with previous versions and that this is unacceptable. What do you do? Throw out the work you've done and start over using another option? Forge ahead and build some sort of compatibility tool later? Why not do a little extra work up front to prevent this from happening in the first place?

### Step 3.4—Identify dependencies for each option pair

*What is a dependency?*

As stated earlier, a dependency is a condition that must be satisfied before a next step can proceed. For software project planning, the condition can be the start or finish of a task, the completion of an entire project, the availability of a certain piece of hardware, the hiring of a software developer, the availability of an existing staff member, and so forth.

*Different kinds of dependencies*

**Start-to-start**

A task that has a start-to-start dependency cannot begin until the condition on which it depends begins.

**Start-to-finish**

This type of dependency is where a task cannot finish until its dependent condition starts.

**Finish-to-start**

The finish-to-start dependency is the most common and the one that you are probably most familiar with. With such a dependency, a task cannot start until the condition it is dependent on finishes.

**Finish-to-finish**

With a finish-to-finish dependency, a task cannot finish until its dependent condition finishes.

### Step 3.5—Specify test requirements for each option pair

Without a detailed design, it will not be possible to create a detailed test specification for each option. At this point, however, it is possible to identify the classes of testing and the types of tests that will be needed to verify that a particular option satisfies quality requirements for the project. The classes and types needed can vary dramatically between options. Consequently, this information can have a significant impact on the option chosen.

The sections below offer examples of well-known and often-used classes and types.

*Test classes*

Testing can be classified as one of the following: testing what's new, regression testing, and integration testing. For each class of testing performed, one or more types of tests will be necessary. More on this in the next section.

Testing what's new

The kind of change proposed by a particular option determines the class of testing that must be performed. In some cases, unit testing will be sufficient. In other cases, unit through scenario tests will be necessary. Given the choice between two functional/design options where one requires unit testing and the other requires unit through scenario testing, the lesser amount of testing required might sway you toward the former option if testing resources or time are scarce.

Regression testing

Regression testing is testing performed to ensure that a change does not have unintended side effects with respect to the product being developed, i.e., that everything that used to work still does.

Integration testing

Integration testing is testing performed to ensure that the product being developed operates properly and does not induce unintended side effects when operating as an integral part of or in cooperative partnership with another product.

*Test types*

Tests can be typed as one of the following: unit, component, stress, system, scenario, and other. Unit tests are the simplest kinds of tests while system and scenario tests are the most complex.

Unit

The purpose of a unit test is to test the individual functions that together provide a single application primitive. To thoroughly test an application primitive, a set of unit tests are developed that test the middle and end or boundary cases of this primitive using every combination of the primitive's options followed by testing all error conditions and then exception conditions.

A middle test case is one that uses a value that falls within the middle of a range of possible valid values while end or boundary cases use values that lie at either extremes of that range. A test for an error condition intentionally performs an illegal operation to determine whether the application handles the error appropriately. Finally, an exception test is a test that seeks to cause the application to fail in some non-deterministic way. For example, to test a word processor's save primitive, unit tests might be developed to test whether all combinations of middle values work correctly, followed by all combinations of end or boundary values, then error conditions, and finally exception conditions.

Component

The purpose of a component test is to test a set of logically-related units. Like unit tests, component tests are developed that test the middle and end or boundary cases followed by testing error conditions and then exception conditions.

Stress

The purpose of a stress test is to push a product to its limits and possibly beyond. Such tests often uncover unexpected design and implementation flaws that would otherwise go undetected. For example, memory leaks, race conditions, dead locks, and other similar and difficult-to-find problems are typically uncovered by such testing.

System

The purpose of a system test is to test a set of logically related components. Testing the synergism between components is the goal of a system test. Like its predecessors, system tests are developed that test the middle and end or boundary cases followed by testing error conditions and then exception conditions.

Scenario

The purpose of a scenario test is to model customer configurations and usage.

Other

A number of other types of tests exist such as usability tests, performance analysis tests, and so on.

### Step 3.6—Specify rough time estimate to complete design, implement, and test each option pair

You have everything you need to make a rough estimate of the time it will take to complete the design, implement, and test each option. Using the information you've collected, layout a simple Gantt chart for each option.

The purpose of the rough estimate is twofold: to determine whether the option "fits" within the project timeframe, and to provide a relative measure of time when comparing options. It is not the official time estimate you will use for the project. That estimate falls out of the remaining steps in the planning process. Beware of the "bias" effect when developing the estimates for each option. The bias effect refers to the phenomenon where the software developers (and you) will unconsciously favorably bias estimates toward the options you like the best versus the best options. Conversely, they will negatively bias estimates for the other options.

### Step 3.7—Create the formal technical documentation

*Purpose*

As mentioned earlier, developing a software product involves much more than designing, implementing, and testing code. It also includes designing, implementing, and testing end-user documentation, creating end-user and sales and support training, creating product data sheets, and so on. To create all of that other material, a knowledge transfer between the software developers and everyone else must occur. Can it occur verbally or by using some other informal method? Sure, but you'll end up missing important information and you'll have to repeat yourself many times. Why not communicate it once in such a way that little if anything is missed so that you'll only have to communicate it once? I used to think that software developers skipped this step to maintain job security and that project leaders skipped it because they measured progress by how much code had been written each day. But I have since concluded that the development of formal technical documentation is skipped because it's difficult and unpleasant.

Skipping this step leads to inefficiency and poor results. Both are clearly counter to our goal to create high performance software development teams. Consequently, this step can neither be skipped nor can it be trivialized. There are many ways in which the details of the product's functional and design characteristics can be captured. In the following sections, I review two: classic functional and design documents and the more contemporary uni-specifications that capture both functional and design information.

*Classic functional specifications and design specifications*

The classic definition of a functional specification is a document that specifies the external interfaces and observable behaviors of a program or program modules.

Design specifications are traditionally divided into a high-level and a low-level specification. The classic definition of a high-level design specification is a document that defines the architecture of a program or program modules without detailing the internal interfaces and algorithms that will ultimately be used for implementation. The low-level specification details the latter.

Byproducts of the waterfall process model

The waterfall process model is a software development model with discreet non-repeating phases that lead from requirements definition to functional specification to design specification to test. More about this process model and others is covered in the Appendix of this book. The byproduct of each phase is a document or set of like documents. In theory, the documents produced by a phase are standalone. Additionally, the documents are static, i.e., once signed-off at the end of the development phase in which they are written, they are seldom if ever updated.

*Contemporary uni-specifications*

Contemporary uni-specifications include all of the information that the classic specifications include. The main differences are that all of the information found in the classic specifications is contained in a single document and that the document is a dynamic document. It's not simply a concatenation of the classic documentation. The information is organized around individual project objectives. The document moves through the development process and appropriate information is updated.

Supports waterfall and other process models, e.g., staged, iterative, and so on.

Although this method of documenting the software development aspects of the project supports the waterfall model, it lends itself to less serial models, e.g., staged, iterative, and so forth.

## Example 5-1: Uni-Specification

### 1.0 OBJECTIVE

(Derived from Requirement 5.1.3) Reduce the number of defects related to the loss of operational data within the system by eliminating those defects involving general system failures.

**Example 5-1: Uni-Specification** 71

## 2.0 ANALYSIS

Upon further investigation and analysis it was determined that the root cause of the general system failures is due to the use of asynchronous thread cancellation.

### *2.1 Background Information*

The POSIX threads pthread_cancel() function is used to terminate threads (others or self). The threads themselves can request how a cancel issued against them should be handled:

1. Check for termination whenever the thread makes a pthreads library call; if there is a pending cancel, the thread terminates.
2. Ignore cancellation requests.
3. Asynchronous cancel that allows the thread to terminate at its earliest convenience.

The pthread's library that Entropy depends on has an unreliable implementation of option 3 above. According to the documentation, use of asynchronous pthreads cancellation is only reliable when using runtime functions documented to be asynchronous cancel safe.

## 3.0 FUNCTIONAL DESIGN (EXTERNAL)

N/A

## 4.0 HIGH-LEVEL DESIGN (INTERNAL)

There are two design options:

1. Wrap all non-asynchronous cancel safe functions to make them safe.
2. Examine each and every use of pthread_setasynccancel() and come up with an alternative solution.

A casual sweep of the source base turned up only a handful of places where we rely on pthread_setasynccancel(). They can be grouped as such:

- Waiting in a select() with infinite (or practically infinite) timeout. Solution: lower timeout, use pthread_testcancel() to see if we are to be terminated, repeat as needed.
- Waiting in a blocking read() or write() Solution: Use the non-blocking functions from the runtime instead, with reasonable timeouts in a loop alternating a timed I/O operation and pthread_testcancel().

## 5.0 LOW LEVEL DESIGN/IMPLEMENTATION DETAILS

TBD

## 6.0 DEPENDENCIES

TBD

## 7.0 TEST REQUIREMENTS

TBD

## 8.0 TIME ESTIMATES

For design option 1, estimates are as follows:

Design: 1 week
Implement: 2 days
Test: 8 days

---

*Which kind of documentation should you use?*

Both methods work, but my experience has been that the latter works better for these reasons:

1. Easier to manage a single document.
2. Single source of information, i.e., all that there is to know about a project deliverable can be found in one place—makes it easier to find the information that you are looking for.
3. When a design changes, function often changes as well and vice versa—having both in the same document makes it easier keep them up-to-date when one or the other is changed.

### Step 4—Select functional/design options

At this point, your options abound. But, how do you select the best options from this collection? Here's where things can get a bit subjective and often emotional for software developers in particular because the best option isn't always the best design. To maintain a degree of objectivity, I suggest you apply the following process:

1. Gather up the project team (not just the software developers, but the entire team that includes representatives from all functions) to review,

Example 5-1: Uni-Specification 73

rate, and select options from the options set. To keep the review focused, limit it to the options presented, i.e., do not open the review to new ideas and suggestions for other options.

2. For each objective, ask all team members to rate each functional/design option on a scale from 1 to 10 where 1 is the worst option and 10 is the best option. Their rating should be based on their answers to these questions:

   How well does the option...

   ... fit the project theme relative to the other options?

   ... fit the project time frame relative to the other options?

   ... satisfy the objective relative to the other options?

3. Calculate average scores and then select the highest scoring options.

4. Break all ties by having team members pick only one of the options and then select the highest scoring option.

**Step 5—Derive major tasks from selected functional/design options**

*Step 5.1—For each option, identify all major tasks that must be completed to implement the option*

This is the first step in an iterative process that is very much like the structured programming technique of functional decomposition with step-wise refinement. Begin the process by selecting one of the functional/design options from Step 4. On the first of a series of passes, break it down into a series of specific work items or tasks that must be completed to fully implement the option. As a rule of thumb, for longer duration options, i.e., options that have been estimated to take more than a man-year to implement, the granularity of this series of tasks should be in the many-months range. For shorter duration options, a many-weeks to a couple of months may be more appropriate.

*Step 5.2—Iterate over the list, further decomposing it until the granularity of tasks is one week or less*

Regardless of the estimated duration of a particular option, any task estimated to take longer than a week can and should be further decomposed until all subtasks are at least a week or less in duration. At this level of detail, it is unlikely that anything of significance has been unaccounted for in the plan. Consequently, the plan has a high degree of accuracy providing a much greater likelihood of a successful outcome.

### Step 6—Identify dependencies

#### *Intra-project dependencies*

Dependencies that are confined to the boundaries of a particular project are called intra-project dependencies. The identification of task dependencies within the confines of a particular project is relatively easy to understand and perform reasonably well. Most often missed, though, is the identification of resource dependencies.

#### *Inter-project dependencies*

Dependencies that transcend project boundaries are inter-project dependencies. These are the most overlooked and typically involve a resource dependency rather than a task dependency.

### Step 7—Identify the critical path

#### *What is the critical path?*

The critical path is the path formed by the series of tasks linked through dependency relationships that must be completed on time for the project to finish on time. The expression "critical path" is really a misnomer. In reality, there may be a number of different converging paths that make up the critical path. The critical path for the project represented by Figure 3-1 is marked by the grey task bars in Figure 5-4.

The critical path tends to stay in a state of flux during a project. In other words, tasks on the critical path at the start of a project don't necessarily stay on the critical path. Conversely, tasks that weren't on the critical path at the start of the project may end up on the critical path.

#### *What is its significance?*

The completion of a project is driven by the critical path. The best way to ensure that a project completes on time is to closely manage the critical path. That means making sure that tasks on the critical path don't slip, and that the critical path stays up-to-date, i.e., tasks are added to and removed from the critical path as necessary.

### Step 8—Identify "mini-release" points

A mini-release point is a point in the project where a subset of the planned enhancements, bug fixes, new features, and so on are completed, integrated, and tested. You can think of it as a dress rehearsal for the final

Example 5-1: Uni-Specification 75

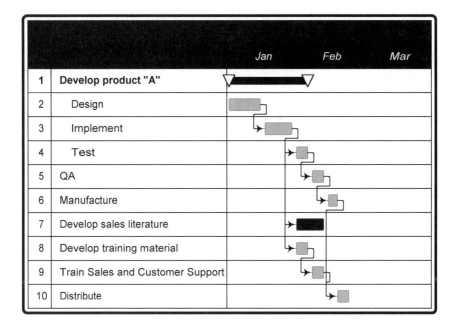

**Figure 5-4** Critical path

integration and test of all planned work for the project. In fact, planned properly, you should be able to release the product at a mini-release point.

A mini-release point serves an important purpose other than giving you an option to release a subset of the product early; it provides a useful early progress indicator. Although the completion of individual tasks on time also serves as an indicator of progress, bringing all of the pieces of the project completed to date and then testing that body of work provides a much more accurate indicator.

### Step 9—Assign people to tasks

#### *Align assignments with interests when possible*

Every software developer I've ever met has an answer to the question, "What do you like to work on the most?" Whether it's the application of object-oriented methodologies, development of three-tier client-server applications, device drivers, or GUIs, every software developer has a passion for something. Aligning assignments with what they are most passionate about will dramatically improve the probability of a successful outcome.

### Tasks as rewards

Rewards take many forms: increased salary, equity in the form of stock grants and options, a night out on the town, and an all-expense-paid vacation. The most popular reward for top performing software developers and leaders of software developers is interesting and challenging work. Each new project presents a potentially rich cache of work that can be assigned to those you wish to reward for past contributions.

### Put your strongest performers on the critical path

Mentioned earlier, the completion of a project is driven by the critical path. Another way to minimize the chances that a task on the critical path slips is to assign critical path tasks to your strongest team members.

## Step 10—Level resources

### Step 10.1—Enforce daily limits

Don't let anyone on the project team work more than some preset daily limit. I've observed, but never measured scientifically, that productivity for a high performer drops off quite dramatically after about 12 hours of non-stop work. Associated with that limit is a contiguous limit of around 10 days. In other words, performance will drop off dramatically after working at the daily limit of 12 hours for more than 10 days in a row.

Software developers use their brains like weightlifters use their muscles. In fact, the brain is like a muscle in that it has a finite capacity to do work and it needs a break in between sets to recover. If you allow your software developers, the high performers that you've hired, to exceed those limits, many will.

### Step 10.2—Balance the workload

Make sure that everyone on the team has roughly the same amount of work. If you let one member of the team or a few carry a load much greater than the rest, you won't achieve the kind of throughput you could otherwise. Balance the workload.

## Step 11—Adjust

### Factor in time constraints (remember that stake in the ground?)

Time is the enemy. Well, perhaps not always. There is one situation where time isn't the enemy: when you have no competition and you don't care if anyone ever buys your product.

Example 5-1: Uni-Specification 77

### Account for attrition

People leave. Eventually they are replaced. But until then, all of their critical path tasks must be reassigned to existing team members whose tasks are not on the critical path to minimize schedule slippage. If the person leaving has no such tasks, then you have the option of deferring reassignment, at least until it looks as if those tasks will wind up on the critical path. When developing the plan, however, it is best to assume the worse. The worst case scenario is that all of the tasks assigned to the people who leave are on the critical path. The simplest way to account for attrition is to assume an average attrition rate and apply it to each task, in effect, amortizing the cost of a worse case attrition scenario across the tasks of all team members. To account for the effect of attrition, increase the time each task will take to complete by the attrition rate, which is calculated by dividing the total number of people assigned to the project at its start by the number of people that you anticipate will be assigned to the project at its finish assuming no replacements.

### Does the plan fit?

If the plan fits, i.e., all tasks can be completed by the target date, then the next step is to execute. Otherwise, you'll have to iterate through the process again starting at Step 4 until you're satisfied with the result.

## Project Planning Tools

There are many project planning tools on the market today. They vary in sophistication from simple single-user single-project tools to complex multiuser multiproject tools. Some display projects in a simple tabular format while others are capable of displaying projects graphically as Gantt and PERT (Program Evaluation and Review Technique) charts. Some allow you to assign resources to tasks, adjust start and stop times of tasks to prevent overloading of resources, consider holidays, perform "what if" analyses, and so on.

My recommendation is that you use a tool that suits the needs of the project. If you are planning a simple project with few tasks and resources, create a spreadsheet with four columns: Task, Resource, Start Date, and Stop Date. For complex projects, choose a more sophisticated tool such as Microsoft Project. For the most complex of projects, you might consider a more sophisticated project management tool.

## The Easy Part Is Done, Time to Execute

The easy part is done. You now have a plan. But remember, it's an 80% plan. In other words, if you make no adjustments to the plan during execution, you'll fulfill approximately 80% of the requirements during the planned time period for the project, or you'll fulfill 100% of the requirements but it will take you 20% longer to complete. To achieve 100%/100%, you'll have to lead, manage, and execute your plan with every ounce of passion you can squeeze out of your heart and soul. You must be as passionate about executing your plan as Romeo was about being with Juliet, Captain Ahab was about slaying the beast Moby Dick, the Wright brothers were about creating a flying machine, Thomas Edison was about inventing a better incandescent light bulb, and Einstein was about finding a unified theory of relativity. You must execute with passion!

# CHAPTER 6

# Execute with Passion

## Execute . . .

### Keep It Simple

Just about everybody has heard the expression "Keep it simple, stupid" better known by its acronym KISS. And few will challenge the corollary to this expression known as the law of complexity—the more complex a system the greater the likelihood it will fail. Insist that everything you do, whether it's designing a user interface, an architecture for a server, or a new process, is as simple as possible. The less complex, the greater likelihood that you'll succeed at achieving your objectives.

### Work Your Project Plan

I'm always amazed when I see someone put a great deal of time and effort into developing a project plan only to shelve it and manage the project as if there were no plan at all. The project plan is your guide. Use it.

#### Lessons from SCUBA diving

One of my hobbies is teaching SCUBA diving. I'm a PADI Open Water SCUBA Instructor. One of the most important subjects we teach during our entry-level course is dive planning. The message is simple: plan your dive and dive your plan. For a SCUBA diver, failure to plan a dive properly and failure to execute to the plan can lead to serious injury or death. Failing to plan a software development project and not following that plan may not lead to injury or death, but success is dependent on doing both. The message is simple: plan your project and follow your plan.

### The changing critical path

You may recall the definition of critical path: "The critical path is the path formed by the series of tasks linked through dependency relationships that must be completed on time for the project to finish on time." In other words, if tasks along the critical path slip, the project will slip. Effective management of the critical path is essential.

The critical path can change for a variety of reasons. Most notably: late tasks, new unplanned tasks, and new unplanned dependencies.

#### Late tasks

Estimates are imprecise. The accuracy of an estimate is directly related to the experience and track record of the estimator and their familiarity with the problem being solved. For example, if the estimator is experienced and has a good track record but has no experience solving a particular type of problem, both the accuracy of the task breakdown and associated times to complete each task will be questionable. Consequently, it is likely that the solution to that particular problem will be late. If those tasks lie on the critical path, the overall project will slip. If they don't, and slip enough, they will form a new critical path. To help you keep an eye on tasks that are most likely to end up on the critical path, color code tasks in the following way:

- Green—task has accurate estimate
- Yellow—estimate is questionable—may go critical
- Red—task is on the critical path

#### Unplanned tasks

No matter how hard you try to identify every task for a project ahead of time, you won't. In fact, you shouldn't try. During the course of a project, new tasks will appear for a variety of reasons from the unseen tasks hidden within a planned task, to the unforeseen task, to tasks associated with new or changing requirements. Regardless of their origin, they will appear and some will end up on the critical path or even create new critical paths.

### Unplanned dependencies

Like unplanned tasks, unplanned dependencies appear for a variety of reasons. Some are missed during the initial development of the plan, others will need to be added to connect unplanned tasks to planned tasks, and some will need to be added to account for new resource dependencies caused by attrition.

### Keep your weakest performers off the critical path

If you want to sleep at night, keep your weakest performers off the critical path. You learned in Chapter 5 that during the initial planning phase you should assign your strongest performers to critical path tasks. But, the critical path will change over the course of the project. Does that mean that if a weak performer ends up on the critical path during the performance of a task you should substitute someone else mid-task? Maybe. More importantly, though, it means that you should prevent it from happening in the first place.

## Maintain Focus

Ultimately, your success depends on your ability to get results. Anything and everything that you do must clearly and indisputably contribute to the attainment of the results that you desire. In your project plan, the desired results are expressed as objectives. Maintain focus by underscoring the fundamental goal: meet or exceed all of the objectives, and insist that team members engage in only those activities that clearly and indisputably contribute to that end.

### Ask questions

You may recall from the Introduction that software developers are curious, consequently, they are easily distracted. Distraction leads to loss of focus. If left unchecked, loss of focus leads to missing objectives and thus low performance. Focus, in this context, refers to working on only those things that contribute to meeting or exceeding all of the objectives for the project.

You can use a simple technique to help your team maintain focus by regularly asking all team members two questions: "What are you working on?" and "Why?" If after asking these questions a few times and they respond in a way that indicates they are focused, then you can reduce the frequency. But don't stop asking altogether. Even the most focused software developer will get distracted from time-to-time.

Of course, asking too often can be perceived as micro-management. I haven't met a software developer yet who likes being micro-managed. If you have a reputation for this, then stop. You'll drive away your best people if you don't.

### Encourage

Encouragement is a powerful tool. What does it mean to encourage someone? It means to impart courage. Courage is that inner strength you draw upon to help you overcome the often arresting side effect of fear of the unknown. It is often fear of the unknown or uncertainty about whether you're doing the right thing that slows or halts progress toward objectives. Maintain focus by reassuring those who you are encouraging that they are on the right track.

### Motivate

In addition to providing encouragement, it's also important to motivate team members. By motivate, I'm referring to the things that you do as the team's leader to lift the spirits of individual team members, ultimately enhancing their performance and collectively the performance of the team. All other things being equal, a spirited team will perform better than a team that lacks motivation. In other words, they are more likely to remain focused on their objectives. How do you motivate your team members?

#### *It's the little things that count*

Most managers look for grand ways to motivate team members. They have contests where they pit them against each other and where the prize is something significant such as a new car, a Caribbean cruise, or a large cash bonus to name a few. The problem with this approach is that there are few winners and many losers. Does being a loser motivate you? Probably not.

Everyone has to feel like a winner. And, chances are you can't afford to give everyone a car. In addition, although it might be great to win a car, it won't motivate everyone. It's important to understand what motivates each person on the team. The only way to figure that out is to get to know each of them. Understand their needs and wants, likes and dislikes, and their dreams and aspirations. Tailor what you do to what you know about that person.

Finally, keep it small. No cars or cruises or big cash bonuses. In fact, for some an occasional pat on the back or thank you goes much further.

### *It's an everyday thing*

If you're not doing it already, make this a priority and practice it everyday. Walk around the office, sit down with your team members one-on-one, and get to know them. Look for ways and opportunities to lift their spirits. It's like building and maintaining a fire. Once you start a fire, you have to tend to it otherwise it will die down and eventually go out. Instead, create and maintain a raging inferno.

### Reward focusing behaviors

Recognize those who assist you with maintaining focus. For example, when a senior member of your team provides encouragement to a junior member who may be uncertain about how best to implement a particular product feature, appropriately acknowledge the senior member's role in helping to maintain focus. Another team member might be adept at seeing obstacles well in advance of encountering them. Yet another might be skilled at finding creative ways to clear those obstacles. All are examples of focusing behaviors.

### Reward results

For a high performance software development team, the only thing that matters in the end is results. Reward the teams that get them.

### Clear the path ahead

### *Prevention*

Obstacles will stand between you and your objectives. Going over, around, or through an obstacle is much harder than preventing them from occurring in the first place. Below are a number of common obstacles and preventative measures.

### *Attrition*

People quit for a reason. I have heard many reason over the years and have concluded that most often people quit a job because (1) they aren't interested in being a part of fulfilling the company's vision or there is no vision, (2) the opportunity before them, i.e., job content, is unappealing, and/or (3) they're being poorly paid.

Another reason people quit is because some need is left unsatisfied. More often then not, the need that is unsatisfied is the need to feel a sense of common purpose.

*Opportunity*

Each and every one of us wants something out of our jobs. For some it's financial gain, for others it's challenging work, and for others it's advancement to greater levels of responsibility. The list is long. Some people quit when they're not getting what they want out of their jobs. Others remain, but effectively quit by working well below what they are capable of. Still others remain, sharing their dissatisfaction with coworkers compounding lowered productivity.

It's important, therefore, to understand what each member of your team wants out of their job. Never assume that you know; always ask. Once you know, work with them to help them achieve what they want. There will be occasions when a member of your team will want something that you will never be able to provide or the timeframe in which you could provide it are well outside of their tolerance. For those cases, it is best for the team member, the rest of the team, and the company for them to move on to something new.

*Compensation*

I haven't met a person yet who likes to be paid less than they are worth. Pay your people what they are worth and then some. Never let compensation be an issue.

*Failure to manage up*

Your long-term success depends on your ability to not only effectively lead your team, but also, your ability to effectively lead the organization. That means you need the ability to lead your superiors as well as your subordinates. The best way to approach this is to look at all of them as peers.

*Failure to manage expectations*

As a product development leader, there is often a gap between what you are actually developing and what others think you are developing. If this gap is wide, then at the conclusion of a product development effort, others will perceive that you have failed. Thus others will view you and your team as poor performers. To prevent this from happening, you must set expectations. This is best achieved through proper planning and communication of those plans.

*Poor morale*

What causes it?

Poor morale is a side effect of doing many things poorly. It can be pervasive, i.e., a side effect of the company performing poorly. Or, it can be isolated to a group, i.e., a side effect of a poorly performing team.

How do you recognize it?

Poor morale typically manifests itself as complaining. Most people complain when things are going poorly. They want change. They want the situation to improve, but don't necessarily know how to improve it. To say, "Don't come to me with your problems, bring me solutions" is telling your team to complain behind closed doors. Then you never hear the complaints and think all is well when in fact what you have is a cancerous growth that will spread through the organization with obvious consequences.

How can you fix it?

If your company or team is performing poorly, throwing a party may ease the pain briefly, but it won't last. The best way to improve morale is to improve performance. The best way to do that is to follow all of the advice I've given you in this book about creating high performance teams.

### Overcome

Unless you're clairvoyant, you won't anticipate every obstacle that may find its way between you and your objectives. When they appear, clear them. Either go around, over, or through them.

### Accept no excuses

Everyone makes excuses. It's a learned behavior that we as humans use to avoid the uncomfortable emotion known as embarrassment. When something goes wrong and you're to blame, the excuse-making behavior is triggered. The good news is that this behavior is relatively easy to spot in others. The bad news is that it's hard to spot in yourself. In either case, it can be unlearned. To start the unlearning process, make it clear to your team that excuses will not be tolerated. When you see it in action, expose it and reiterate that you will not tolerate it. It's important to remember that an excuse is only an excuse when the person (or people) making it are the cause of the failure. If a failure can be attributed to something outside of their control, then it's not an excuse.

Warning: when someone accepts responsibility for a failure, don't punish them. Instead, work with them to make certain that the failure does not recur. Permitting a recurring failure is not acceptable.

### Manage performance

#### *Performance appraisals*

*Purpose*

A performance appraisal is a critique of one's performance over some period. They are generally administered on an arbitrary date, i.e., one's employment anniversary, semi-annually, or quarterly, and contain a potpourri of performance measures. In my opinion, they are an ineffective management tool.

For a high performance software development team, all that matters is whether the team meets or exceeds its objectives. To that end, a performance appraisal must be concerned primarily with project execution. Tasks, behaviors, focus areas, and the like that may be appropriate for one project may not be appropriate for others. A performance appraisal should answer the question, "What have you done to contribute to or detract from achieving or exceeding the objectives of the project?" To answer that question, the performance appraisal cycle must coincide with a project cycle. At the start of the project, each team member should know what he or she must contribute to the project and how that contribution will be measured. Likewise, the team must know what it has to do be successful.

Unfortunately, performance appraisals are more often used as a tool to find fault rather than celebrate success and focus on growth. When used as a fault-finding device, they can easily destroy one's confidence and sap motivation. Instead, use them to drive improvement.

*Frequency*

Every member of the team should know at all times what is expected of them with respect to objectives and the measures of success. That means that appraising performance is a near daily activity. Start by writing down what is expected. Deliver it. Frequently monitor progress. Correct as needed.

### *Performance plans*

#### *Purpose*

A performance plan complements the appraisal process in that it reinforces what was done well during previous appraisal periods, highlights areas that need improvement or further development, and suggests ways to effect those improvements all within the context of what is needed to make the next project a success, i.e., achieve or exceed project objectives.

#### *Frequency*

A performance plan must be developed at the beginning of a project. Develop and execute the plan as you would any other; execute with passion.

### *Performance problems*

While monitoring performance and working a performance plan, you will find problems. The way I approach resolving performance problems is quite simple. It is a four-step process: coach, counsel, correct, and terminate.

#### *Step 1—Coach*

Coaching is an effective way to steer someone away from a performance problem. If you notice that a member of your team or the team as a whole is heading toward a performance problem, nudge them away from it. Coaching is subtle. When coaching, you reveal obstacles that lie ahead and give those you are coaching the opportunity to plot a course around the obstacle. If they falter, walk them through the process of plotting a new course then back away and let them follow through.

#### *Step 2—Counsel*

If you observe that a member of your team is performing poorly in some area, get with them, let them know, and explain how they can correct the problem. If the team is performing poorly in some area, get them all together in a room and counsel them as a team. When performance problems are caught and corrected early, more drastic measures can often be avoided.

#### *Step 3—Correct*

Correcting a performance problem that could not be handled through counseling requires greater planning and formality. A good way to handle such situations is to develop a plan for the poor performer that clearly articulates the problem and explains what they must do to turn the situation around. It should be specific and measurable. If the performance problem is severe, you may need to further explain that failure to correct in some reasonable period of time will result in more drastic measures.

*Step 4—Terminate*

The ultimate measure to take is firing a poor performer. It is one of the most difficult challenges you will ever face as a manager. There are social, moral, and ethical issues to consider. Great care should be taken to ensure that all other courses of action have been explored. If it is your only remaining option, then carry it out swiftly and as painlessly as possible to both you and the person you are letting go.

## . . . With Passion

### Think Like a Winner

In American culture, winning is the overarching goal of all endeavors. Of course, winning is relative. It could mean that you're the biggest, fastest, or the best at something, or that you have the most of something, and so on. The desire to win is learned at an early age and reinforced throughout life.

In business, winning is about having dominant market share, being profitable, and having greater revenue than your competitors. It can also be about having the best product on the market, or the best service. Regardless, winning is fleeting. It is a moment in time. Once that moment is gone, the door is open for someone else to win and for you to lose. How do you gain and maintain a winning position?

### Set high standards

If you want to win and stay a winner, your standards must be higher than your competitors'. In fact, they must be much higher. Keep the gap as wide as possible to make it difficult for them to catch up to you.

### Push the limits

There are two kinds of limits: real and perceived. Everybody thinks they know their own limits, but chances are, they really don't. One kind of limit, perceived, is when you think you've reached your limit. The other kind, real, is when you've actually reached your limit. Pushing yourself to your real limit spurs growth. Growth leads to new levels of performance, which leads to winning. Continuous growth leads to keeping the gap between you and your competitors wide.

### Lessons from Basic Training

I spent the summer after my senior year in high school attending U.S. Army Basic Training at Fort Jackson, South Carolina. It was there that I learned the difference between perceived and real limits. I could give many examples, but one in particular stands out. The Army requires every soldier to pass a physical readiness test. This includes some basic measures of physical conditioning. For example, you must be able to run two miles, perform a certain number of push ups, and so on. During one such test, I was struggling to perform the minimum number of push ups required to pass. My drill instructor was no help—he taunted me, trying to convince me to quit. But my will to succeed helped me to overcome the pain I was experiencing. I discovered that despite the pain, I could do more.

## Create a Sense of Urgency

### What is it?

What does it mean to have a sense of urgency? It means being in a perpetual race against time while focused like a laser beam on reaching your objectives.

### What happens if you don't have it?

A lack of urgency is cancer to an organization. Depicted graphically, the performance over time of an organization that lacks a sense of urgency against a competitor with a sense of urgency is shown in Figure 6-1.

The performance over time of an organization that has a sense of urgency against a competitor that lacks a sense of urgency is shown in Figure 6-2.

### How do you create it?

#### Artificial—temporary

There are a variety of ways that you can create a temporary sense of urgency. All are easy to apply and can be effective short-term methods. None of them, however, are effective long-term methods because once you stop applying a particular method, the sense of urgency disappears.

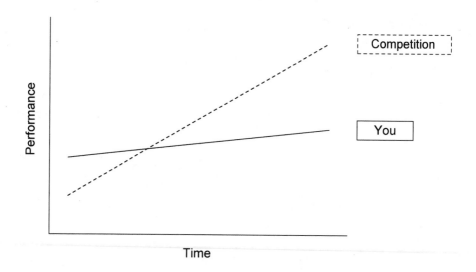

**Figure 6-1** The long-term effect of lack of urgency on performance.

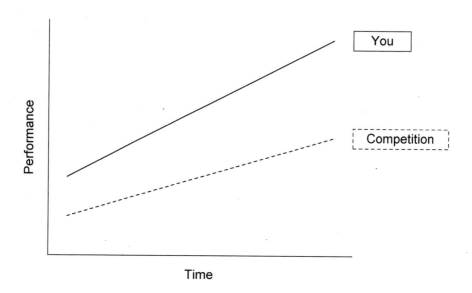

**Figure 6-2** The long-term effect of maintaining a strong sense of urgency on performance.

### Incentives

Incentives are a time-honored tool for getting someone to do something extraordinary. My wife used to work for a company that raffles expensive sports cars as part of an extraordinarily aggressive recruiting program. Sales people at my last company know all about incentives; once they exceed their quota, special commission rates kick in to encourage ever greater revenue generation. Stock options are another kind of incentive that ties you to future performance of the company. The better the company does, the higher the stock price, the more money you make.

Unfortunately, it's typically during those times when you need your team to have the greatest sense of urgency around a particular objective that you can't afford incentives such as those already mentioned.

### Threats

There's nothing like a good old threat when you need something done in a hurry. How's this for an urgency provoking threat: "If you fail to deliver that new product by the first of next month, your employment will be terminated." Or perhaps something like this: "If you fail to exceed your quota by 10% this quarter, we'll have to lay off a few people; their livelihood is in your hands." Another one: "If sales don't increase by a factor of two next quarter, we'll have to close our doors!"

It's certainly an effective method for getting results quickly, but at what cost? I haven't met a person yet who enjoyed working in an environment where threats were the norm. Sooner or later, they will leave, which will put a greater burden to perform on those left behind. Consequently, more threats will be issued driving away others. With the attrition rate skyrocketing, the organization will eventually wither and die.

### Natural – permanent

Imagine if everyone on your team had an ever-present and natural sense of urgency and that you never had to resort to any of the short-term urgency-provoking methods covered in the last section. Just imagine the energy you'd feel in the halls of such an organization and the kind of performance you could realize with a team full of people who had a natural sense of urgency. Imagine an environment where the use of incentives, threats, and other forms of artificial urgency-provoking techniques were unnecessary. Sounds too good to be true? Although rare, such environments do exist. But they just don't happen. They are created and maintained.

Take a look around your organization. Does anyone stand out as someone with a true sense of urgency? Do you know anyone who occasionally exhibits behaviors characteristic of someone with a sense of urgency but not consistently? Do you know anyone who doesn't exhibit it at all? Every organization will have some mix of all three. How do you create an organization that has most, if not all, of the former and none of the latter? Creating one starts by classifying members of your organization as having one of three degrees of urgency: full, partial, and spectator. It ends with leveraging the strengths of the former, drawing out the potential of the next, and weeding out the latter.

### Full

I was at a restaurant recently with my wife when I accidentally knocked over a glass of wine. As it spread out over the table approaching its edge, we both jumped to our feet and backed away to avoid getting soiled. Our response to this event was reflexive. In other words, nobody needed to yell at us to jump out of the way of the approaching wine, nor did either of us consciously think about getting out of the way; we simply reacted. This reaction to a threatening situation, i.e., the fight or flight response, is a built-in, or innate, part of who we are as human beings. Similarly, some people possess an innate sense of urgency. Nobody has to tell them to act urgently; they simply do.

### Partial

Others, are capable of experiencing a sense of urgency but only when provoked, asked to, or as a side effect of someone else's display of urgency. During my wine spilling experience, I called our waiter over to the table to assist us with cleanup. His slow and deliberate stroll to our table quickly turned to a fast walk as I frantically flagged him over. The excited look on my face, the fact that my wife and I were standing at our table rather than sitting, and my frantic waving all helped to induce a sense of urgency in him. Clearly, he was capable of experiencing urgency but didn't until provoked.

### Spectator

Curiously, nobody around us who had witnessed the event came to our aid. My display of urgency did not provoke anyone in the vicinity of the event. They were spectators, watching the whole scene unfold as if they were sitting on their couch at home glued to a mind-numbing television show. No doubt you have people in your organization who stand by on the sidelines watching rather than actively participating in the game. They are the spectators. Since they are not in the game, they cannot display a sense of urgency about it. They may comment and criticize, playing "arm chair quarterback" but never directly engage. Get rid of them.

# CHAPTER 7

# Conclusion

Now you know everything I know about creating high performance software development teams. Hopefully, it all seems reasonable to you and that, if nothing else, you picked up a good tip or two. In a couple of places in the book, I've used acronyms to help you remember key elements of this methodology. Here's one last memory aid to help you recall the steps that I believe must be followed to create such teams: Run Time Problems Plague Execution where R stands for Requirements, T stands for Team, P stands for Prepare, the other P stands for Plan, and E stands for Execute. The following sections summarize each.

## Nail Down the Requirements

Requirements must answer these basic questions: What problem will the product solve? How will the product solve the problem? Who has the problem? When do they need a solution? Finally, is it worth building? The answers to these questions form the foundation upon which everything else that follows—building the team, preparing the team, planning, and execution—is built. Just like a house is only as good as its foundation, a software product is only as good as its requirements.

## Build the Best Team

How do you build a high performance software development team when its members think like computers, don't like being told what to do or how to do it, and whose curiosity often leads them astray? Start by hiring the right talent.

Don't approach hiring as if it were a numbers game, a slot-filling exercise, or a race against time. You will achieve much better results if you focus on hiring people who match your needs rather than simply hiring to fill an opening in your organizational chart or hiring to beat a hiring deadline. Start by creating a hiring profile that defines your ideal candidate across these dimensions: (1) cultural fit, (2) personality, (3) track record, and (4) knowledge, skills, and experience.

The way your team is organized also plays a crucial role in whether it is successful. Traditional organizational structures aren't optimized for high performance.

## Prepare the Team

If our world were ideal, you'd always find people who exactly match the profile of the person that you're looking for. Reality, of course, is that such people are rare. More often than not, they have too much or not enough of what you're looking for. At a minimum, to create a high performance software development team, you must hire someone who is a close cultural and personality match with your hiring profile and who has a solid track record of accomplishment. A mismatch there cannot be corrected.

## Prepare to Lead

To effectively lead a team you must remember that you are leading people. People are complex far beyond the most complex machines ever devised. Treat them like machines and you will achieve suboptimal results.

There is a difference between leading and managing. Leading people is fundamentally about pulling them toward their objectives. Managing people is about pushing them there. High performance teams are lead not managed. Are you a manager or a leader? If you're not a leader, become one.

## Planning

Planning is boring to software developers. They want to design and code. To make matters worse, operating without a plan, by the seat of your pants, adds an element of risk and excitement to a project that appeals to many software developers, particularly those with a strong entrepreneurial spirit.

The worst case is no plan at all. Lacking any specific objectives such projects are doomed to fail. The next best case is a plan that enumerates objectives but does not lay out a clear and well thought out course that maps how to get from where you are to where you want to go. Next is a proper plan with objectives and a well-designed course that isn't followed. Finally, there's the proper plan that is followed. This plan leads to high performance.

Planning is best approached following an 80/20 rule; aim for 80% accuracy in the first cut of the plan and refine it toward 100% during execution.

## Execute with Passion

Nailing down the requirements, hiring the right talent, organizing for success, preparing your team, learning how to lead, and planning culminates with execution. All of the hard work that went into getting to this point can easily be undone. How do you prevent that from happening? You have a plan, *follow it*. In the end, it's all about execution.

# Developing Software

## Software Development Processes

A process defines a sequence of steps to perform to achieve some end. There are many different types of processes followed within the software industry. For example, most software development organizations follow what is called the waterfall process. Other popular processes include prototyping and iterative. There are a number of others, however, these are the most common and are discussed in detail below.

### Types of Software Development Processes

#### Waterfall

The waterfall process consists of a number of phases where the activities performed during each phase are logically related and unique with respect to the activities performed in other phases. Each phase is distinct; in other words, it has an identifiable beginning and ending as shown in Figure A-1.

Strictly followed, once a phase has been completed, it is never repeated. During the first phase, or analysis phase, the product requirements, development plan, and the test, QA, documentation, and manufacturing plans are developed. During the second phase, the product is designed. The primary activity in the third phase is implementation of the design. And, finally, the implementation is tested in the fourth phase.

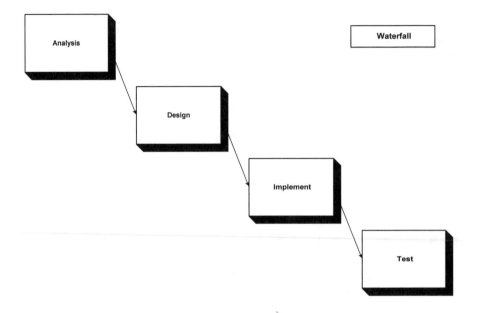

**Figure A-1**   Waterfall

## Prototyping

The prototyping process is the waterfall process preceded by a phase where a working model of the system is developed. A working model is a model that, to the user, looks and operates like the real thing. However, internally, the prototype may be incomplete or in some non-final form. The prototype is developed to validate the requirements and to test design options before proceeding with the development of the final requirements, design, and implementation as shown in Figure A-2.

Some followers of this process believe that the prototype must be disposed of following its completion. Others, like myself, believe that at least parts of the prototype can be reused in the final product.

This process attempts to overcome the primary weakness of the waterfall process; that the requirements for the system must be completely defined before moving on to the next phase in the development cycle. Development of a prototype gives an organization a means to refine and, hopefully, completely specify the requirements for the system. Once the requirements are

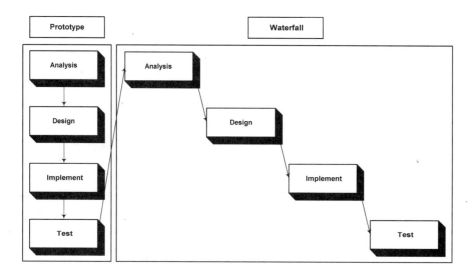

**Figure A-2** Prototyping

completely specified, development of the real thing can proceed by following the traditional waterfall process.

## Iterative

Unfortunately, more often than not, development of the prototype does not provide enough information to develop a complete specification of the requirements. Consequently, the prototype process breaks down during later phases when the requirements must be changed. The iterative process evolved from this weakness in the prototyping process.

Like the prototyping process, the iterative process produces a working version of the product during the first phase. Unlike the prototyping process, the end-result of the first phase is not automatically discarded. Also, unlike the prototyping process, the end-result of the first phase is an incomplete, but working subset of the final product. Both internally and externally, the product is in near final-form. On the other hand, in the prototyping process the end-result of the first phase may appear to the user to be complete, but internally may be far from final form.

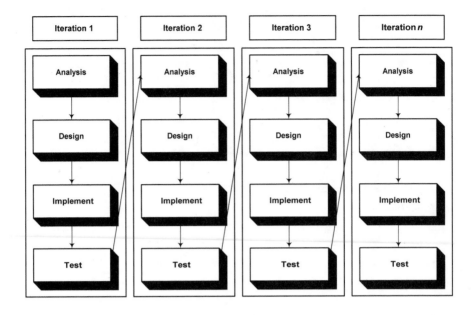

**Figure A-3** Iterative

For the iterative process, each phase following the first is an incremental refinement of its predecessor and there is no fixed limit to the number of iterations that can be performed as shown in Figure A-3. However, too few iterations may degrade the process to either the prototyping or waterfall process. Too many iterations may add unnecessary overhead to the project.

For both the waterfall and prototyping processes to succeed, requirements must be completely specified early in the project. In other words, after the requirements are specified, they must not be changed once the phase during which they are developed has ended. Anyone who has ever developed a complex software application or system will tell you that their requirements are rarely if ever completely specified, for a number of reasons. Some of the more common reasons are:

- Over time, the problem being solved changes.

- The root of the problem being solved is common; however, each user has unique requirements that cannot be determined until the product is deployed.
- The needs and wants of users change, and the technology used to solve the problem changes at a rate that quickly makes a solution obsolete.

The advantage of the iterative process over the other two covered in this book is that it is designed to accommodate change, i.e., change in product requirements, change in design, change in implementation, and change in test. It accomplishes this by treating the entire software development process as a series of mini-waterfalls that begins with the development of a subset of the system and from mini-waterfall to mini-waterfall progresses toward what becomes an implementation of the system that satisfies the requirements. The other advantage it has over the other two discussed here is that at the end of each phase, or mini-waterfall, a working, fully-tested subset of the product is available. If, as we will see later, it becomes necessary to release the product before the entire system is implemented, this process can accommodate such a need. The others cannot since an intermediate, fully-tested implementation is not available until the end of the project.

## Selecting the Right Process to Follow

Popular use of the waterfall process for software development can be traced back to the late 60s. Back then, both computers and their software were most often designed to solve specific problems from the venues of mathematics and science. Also, during that period, computing time was expensive, computing resources were limited, and software development tools were either non-existent or primitive. The things that we take for granted today, such as third+ generation languages, source-level debuggers, sophisticated GUIs, and the like, either did not exist or were used infrequently. Software developers had to carefully analyze the requirements, design a solution, and write and test the code by hand to avoid incurring unnecessary computer charges and delays associated with limited resource availability.

As the set of problems solved by software systems expanded from narrow in scope to broad in scope, it became increasingly more difficult to completely specify the requirements for those systems. Consequently, the prototyping process became a popular software development process to follow since it provides a means to validate the requirements, ultimately enabling the development of a more complete requirements specification.

Quite often, though, the prototyping process suffers from the same weakness that the waterfall process suffers from; the requirements for the system cannot be completely specified. The iterative process supports the development of a product where the requirements, design, implementation, and testing undergo a series of refinements that over time lead to a complete specification of the requirements and a product that completely satisfies those requirements.

Selecting the correct process for a product development effort to follow is relatively straightforward. The first step is to identify the scope of the problem. The second step is to factor in the importance of releasing the product at a particular point in time. The third step is to determine whether the tools available for the project will support or compromise the success of the project when following a particular process.

### Scope of problem

The waterfall process works well for cases where the problem to be solved is narrow in scope. Cases that are broad in scope, however, tend to be difficult, if not impossible, to specify completely. Without a complete specification of requirements, the waterfall process quickly breaks down. If the development of a complete requirements specification proves to be impossible, the waterfall process would be a poor choice to follow.

The prototype process model works well for cases where the problem to be solved is broader in scope. Unfortunately, there is no simple way to determine whether the scope of the problem being solved is too large for the prototyping process to be effective. To determine whether the scope is too broad for the prototyping process, you must have a high degree of confidence that the development of a complete specification will be possible following the development of the prototype. If that feeling of confidence is not present, chances are that the scope of the problem is not too broad. If, however, you feel a low degree of confidence that it will be possible to develop a complete specification following the development of the prototype, the scope of the problem is probably too broad.

Finally, the iterative process works well for cases where the problem to be solved is broad in scope and where the development of a complete requirements specification is not possible. This process is specifically designed for such cases. By treating the development process as a series of mini-waterfalls that are repeatedly refined, the end result is the development of an application or system that solves the problem as specified by the requirements.

### Schedule

Another factor that must be considered when selecting a process is project schedule. For the waterfall process, the project schedule is usually set during the first phase. For the prototyping process, the project schedule is usually set following the development of the prototype. And, for the iterative process, the project schedule is usually set early but revised repeatedly along with the other project deliverables. Regardless of which process is followed, it is often the case that the date selected is arbitrary. Other times, the date selected lies within what is called a market window of opportunity. The market window of opportunity for a product is the period of time during which demand for the product is predicted to be at its highest. Hitting the window at the right moment is crucial to acquiring the greatest share of the market. Accurate project schedules, therefore, are extremely important. Unfortunately, both the waterfall and prototyping processes have poor track records for predicting when a project will finish.

Why do these two processes consistently fail to accurately predict project schedule? The main reason is that if during a downstream phase, a problem is encountered that was introduced in an upstream phase, the only recourse is to return to the upstream phase, resolve the problem, and revisit the phases that follow. When upstream activities are revisited, the changes ripple all the way down to the bottom, ultimately pushing the schedule out. For example, a performance problem discovered during the test phase usually requires a change to the design. Once the design is changed, the code must be changed and the testing repeated. But, since the problem wasn't uncovered until late in the cycle, the schedule slip is at the end of the project often pushing the delivery out beyond the window of opportunity. In other words, changes to the schedule required as a result of having to revisit earlier phases can have a large impact on the overall schedule.

The iterative process isn't necessarily any better at predicting when a project will finish; however, since the schedule goes through a series of refinements like the other project deliverables, the schedule becomes more accurate over time. And, since revisiting an earlier phase is done within the context of a mini-waterfall, the ripple effect is contained and usually has a much smaller effect on the schedule. Also, at the end of each iteration, a working subset of the system is produced. If the schedule is slipping past the window of opportunity, the company has the option to release a subset of the product with the rest to follow in a subsequent release. With the other processes, no such option exists.

When choosing a process to follow, the importance of delivering the product at a particular point in time must be considered. Let's consider some of the combinations. If the problem to be solved is narrow in scope and the window of opportunity is wide, then the waterfall process will suffice. However, if the scope of the problem to solve is broad in scope and the window of opportunity is narrow, your chances of success may increase if you follow the prototyping process. If the scope of the problem to solve is wide and the window of opportunity is also wide then either the prototyping or the iterative processes may work best. Finally, if the scope is wide and the window of opportunity is narrow, then you'll stand a much greater chance of success if you follow the iterative process.

### Availability of tools

The waterfall process was developed during a time when tools in general were relatively unsophisticated. In particular, compiler technology was primitive. Most code was written in assembler. Debuggers were simple and required an in-depth knowledge of the underlying hardware architecture. In those days, debugging was such a painful prospect that code was usually committed to the machine only after being meticulously and painstakingly hand executed. In fact, for the most part, the code was debugged before ever executing on the system for which it was written. The waterfall process is a good match for product development efforts that are constrained to use primitive development tools.

As tools became more sophisticated—in particular, as assembler gave way to third-generation languages like C—and source level debuggers were introduced, less care was necessary during the implementation phase of a product development effort. The pace of software development began to accelerate. It became economical to develop and execute code earlier in the implementation phase since any problems introduced as a result of hastiness could be isolated and removed using a modern debugger. In fact, the economics of code writing was such that working models of the product could be developed to guide the development of the final product or real thing. It was during this period that the prototyping process became popular.

Since then, compiler and debugger technology has advanced to the point that lay people, using this technology, can develop highly sophisticated applications quickly with little training. The cost per line of code, both in terms of dollars and time, has reached such a low point that the development of numerous prototypes during a product development effort has become economical. The iterative process is possible because of the existence of such tools and is just now beginning to gain acceptance as a mainstream software development process.

Most new software development is developed using the latest technologies available. Modern compilers and debuggers make following a process like the iterative process possible. However, there are certainly many new products being developed on legacy systems for which modern compiler and debugger technologies are not available. For such projects, it may not be possible or economically practical to follow the iterative process. Otherwise, all three processes are suitable.

## Configuration Management

A configuration is a particular instance of a product. For example, Microsoft Word 7.0 for Windows 95, the product that I'm using to develop this book, is a particular instance of the Microsoft Word product. Other instances (or configurations) of the product include earlier versions such as version 1.0, 2.0, and so on, and the versions that run under the Apple MacIntosh operating system.

Configuration Management (CM) refers to the set of processes and procedures that an organization follows and the tools that it uses to manage the source code from which various configurations of a product are derived. Management of the source code includes specifying and enforcing such policies as restricting access to certain individuals, preventing more than one person from modifying the same code at the same time, restricting the type of code checked-in to a particular class, i.e., defect repairs versus enhancements, and so on. Management of the source code also includes defining the content of a particular configuration of the product. Once the content is defined, the specific derivative of the product can be produced. Production refers to the activities engaged in and the tools used to construct the product.

Despite what CM tool vendors tell you, CM can be practiced without sophisticated and often expensive tools. However, the larger an organization, the bigger the product, and the greater the number of versions of the product, the harder it is to practice CM without the aid of such tools. Now, for a closer look at the three essential components of CM: source code control, production, and problem/defect tracking.

## Source Code Control

Source code control refers to the act of controlling access to and changes made to a product's source files. Some CM systems provide mechanisms to enforce access policies. For example, a valid defect number from the defect tracking system must be entered before check-out/check-in is permitted, or approval from a higher authority such as a manager or product development change committee must be granted before check-out/check-in is permitted.

Once access to a file is granted, changes to that file can be managed using one of two methods: (1) sequential or (2) copy-merge. For the sequential method, only one person at a time is permitted to modify the file. This restriction is usually enforced by employing a lock mechanism. In other words, when a module or file is checked out of the source code control system, a lock is engaged preventing anyone else from checking-out the same module or file. Once the lock holder checks the file back into the source code control system, the lock is disengaged allowing someone else to check the file out. The positive aspect of the sequential method is that it prevents one person from undoing the work of another. One of its limitations, however, is that anyone else who may need to modify the same file will be blocked until the file is checked in.

For the copy-merge method, many people can independently check-out and modify the same modules or files. As each file is checked-in, however, they must be merged to prevent one person from overwriting changes made by others. For example, imagine that you and I checked-out a file containing the following C function:

```c
int sum(int x, int y)
{
     int z;
     z=x+y;
     return z;
}
```

I decide to change the code to return a 0 if the sum of x and y exceeds 10. My copy of the code now looks like:

```
int sum(int x, int y)
{
     int z;
     z=x+y;
     if (z > 10)
          z=0;
     return z;
}
```

At the same time, you add a line of code to your copy of the original file that will display the sum before returning. Your copy of the code now looks like:

```
int sum(int x, int y)
{
     int z;
     z=x+y;
     printf("%d\n", z);
     return z;
}
```

If I check in my code first, it will take the place of the original. When you check in your code, rather than take the place of my version, it must be merged. In other words, the changes that we made in our copies of the original must be reconciled. Source control systems that support the copy-merge paradigm have tools that automatically merge code in such situations. For this case, the merged code would look like:

```
int sum(int x, int y)
{
     int z;
     z=x+y;
     if (z > 10)
          z=0;
     printf("%d\n", z);
     return z;
}
```

Automatic merging, however, is not foolproof. You should always review the results of a merge to make sure that the tools did not create an abomination. Also, there are times when the tools cannot reconcile the differences between two variants of the original. In such situations, the utilities somehow flag the conflict and hand merging becomes necessary.

The positive aspect of the copy-merge method is that software developers are never blocked. On the other hand, merging is not foolproof and must be reviewed carefully. The time needed to conduct such reviews may negate the benefit of not blocking.

### Production

Production can be divided into two categories: version management and construction. Version management refers to the set of policies and procedures that when enforced, define the specific content of a particular version of the product, i.e., the set of sources needed to construct a particular version of a product. Construction refers to the set of policies and procedures that when followed result in the creation of a specific version of the product. The following two sections address each of these categories in more detail.

### Version Management

As mentioned earlier, version management refers to the set of policies and procedures that control the creation of a particular version of a product. For example, imagine an application that consists of hundreds, if not thousands, of individual source files. During the development of the next major release of the product, existing source files are changed, some may be deleted, and new source files may be added. At some point, a final build of the product is made based on a policy, or set of rules, that defines the specific set of files to be used to produce that specific version of the product.

An example of a version management policy is that maintenance releases will contain only defect repairs made to the product since the last release. Another example: a patch release will contain only the changes made to the product to repair the specific defect that the patch was designed to repair. The procedures followed to enforce such policies vary depending on the CM system being used.

### Construction

Mentioned earlier, construction refers to the set of policies and procedures that when followed result in the creation of the specific version of the product identified through enforcement of the version management policies discussed in the previous section. An example of a construction policy is that products will be built on systems that are used solely for the purpose of constructing the product. Such a policy is designed to prevent the product from being tainted by unofficial or intermediate versions of libraries. For example, the product must be built using an optimizing compiler set at maximum optimization and with full debug information.

## Problem/Defect Tracking

Tracking can be performed using a pad of paper and a pencil, a flat-file, a spreadsheet, or a system designed specifically for problem/defect tracking. The first three can be used for smaller projects and teams. However, for larger projects and teams, a more sophisticated system is almost always a necessity.

Among the systems designed specifically for this task, features sets vary significantly. The simplest of them are best characterized as basic record keeping systems that capture general information. More sophisticated systems include mechanisms that allow you to assign problems/defects to certain individuals who are then automatically notified by e-mail or pager that an assignment has been made. Usually, such systems support some facility to move the defect through various states, e.g., from new to open to resolved to verified. The most advanced systems are integrated with the source code control and production systems and provide ways to link problem/defect reports with source modules and files.

## Quality Assurance

### In the Eyes of the Beholder

Like most software developers, I'm certain that your mind is racing with thoughts of how best to implement that "must have" feature that marketing is pushing for, the defect that was just assigned to you that has to be fixed right this minute to appease an irate customer, and those persistent thoughts about how screwed up management is at your company. And here I am about to ask you to add yet another thought to the pile. So, take a deep breath. Exhale. Now, visualize a quality software product that you've recently purchased. Why is it a quality product? Is it because the developers that made it followed coding standards and held code inspections, or that their organization is registered to ISO 9000, or that they have a corporate policy that required them to eliminate all known defects before shipping the product? Probably not. My bet is that your reply includes statements that have little or nothing to do with processes, procedures, and test results. Taking off your engineer's cap, as a customer, you are more concerned with such things as the product's reliability, availability, performance, and the responsiveness of the company's service and support organizations.

Like you, your customers define quality in terms of attributes that the product and the company producing the product possess, such as easy to use, well packaged, or the company's service and support are impressive. Unfortunately, these quality attributes are often completely ignored by the company developing the product. Instead, the company's QA objectives are set based on an internal definition of quality that is often mandated in a corporate standards document that dictates criteria, such as 85% code coverage and no severity-one defects. (I define a severity-one defect to be a defect where a product feature or function is non-operable.)

If you accept the premise that your customers are the ultimate judge of your product's quality and you don't know their definitions of quality, how can you ever hope to produce a quality product? In this section, I introduce a methodology that I call "Customer Oriented Software Quality Assurance" that is designed to help you build a QA program based first on your customers' definition of quality. For a more in-depth coverage of this topic, refer to my book *Customer Oriented Software Quality Assurance*.[1]

Throughout my career, I have studied and applied a long list of methodologies, techniques, processes, and procedures attempting to produce software products of the highest quality. At some point, I began to ask myself, which one is best. I wanted to settle on a particular one that I could apply over and over again to achieve consistent and desirable results. As I gave this particular problem serious thought, it occurred to me that to achieve this goal I would first have to define "desirable results." Isn't the primary desired result to produce a product of the highest quality? Yes. But, what does that mean? I realized I would have to find the elusive definition of quality before

---

1.    Ginac, Frank P. *Customer Oriented Software Quality Assurance*. Prentice Hall PTR. Englewood Cliffs, NJ: 1997.

I could solve this mystery. This section and the book that it is based on are the end result of that effort. It's not based on extensive research conducted in libraries and research labs. It's based on years of ad hoc research, trial and error, and my personal experiences.

This methodology addresses several common problems faced when producing software products for sale:

- Complex software systems having hundreds of millions of possible test cases and test scenarios are rarely if ever completely tested due to the practical constraints of time and resources. How do you select a sufficient subset of tests and test scenarios so the quality of the end product satisfies your customers?
- Metrics are used throughout the software industry to gauge product quality. For example, the defects per thousand lines of code measurement might have an associated acceptable value of less than one defect per million lines of code. If a product has one defect per 10 thousand lines of code, is its quality poor? How do you select the right metrics to gauge product quality?
- Tests are the primary means by which product quality is assessed. Is the quality of the product poor? Perhaps, but ultimately, the value of a test lies in its ability to determine whether the product satisfies your customers' quality requirements. For example, is a test that places a load on the system five times greater than any customer will ever place on the system a good determinant of quality?

### Quality Attributes

The quality attributes set is a way to represent customer quality. To create the quality attributes set, you must ask both your current and prospective customers to answer a number of questions that collectively ask the question, "How do you define quality?" By consolidating their responses, you will develop the set of quality attributes that describe their quality requirements. Examples of quality attributes are presented next. You must determine the unique quality requirements of your customers.

### Product-specific attributes

#### *Ease of use*

Have you ever used a product that seemed to have more controls than necessary, or controls placed in odd or awkward positions, or perhaps seemed to be missing controls? Have product-use procedures ever baffled you or made you feel like an idiot? Products like the VCR have long had terrible ease-of-use reputations. Have you ever tried to program your VCR to tape a show at a certain time, day, and channel while you're away? If your VCR has on-screen programming then, perhaps, the procedure is tolerable. But, if you have an older VCR, like mine, then you find the task of programming it so counter intuitive and painful that you avoid this feature all together.

If you had to choose between two products that are identical in every way except one is reported to be easy-to-use and the other as difficult, which would you choose? Most would agree that the former would appeal to more customers.

#### *Documentation*

Incomplete, missing, inaccurate, and poorly translated documentation may lead many customers to conclude that a product is of poor quality. Documentation is usually an afterthought in product development efforts. For some of your customers, this may not pose a problem. For others, however, the documentation is a vital part of their daily use of the product.

#### *Defect tolerance*

Put simply, a defect is an undesirable behavior or characteristic of a product. Some defects are more severe than others. For example, you are driving your car down the street and decide to adjust your side-view mirror—you have one of those mechanical mirror adjusters. Suddenly, you hear a snap and the control falls limp in your hand. Time for a new car? Probably not. If you are at all like me, you'll view it as an engineering challenge, a problem to be solved, and run home to open up that old tool box and put your skills as a backyard mechanic to the test. That sort of breakdown, though annoying, is not as severe as say, your engine suddenly seizing.

#### *Defect frequency*

If you determine that a particular kind of defect type is tolerable (you've interviewed your customers who told you they would tolerate such defects) but your customers encounter them in your product with great frequency, the breakdown will likely become intolerable. If a defect becomes intolerable because of a high frequency of incidence, then elimination of these defects should become a priority.

### Organization-specific attributes

#### *Service and support*

Despite all of your efforts to eliminate defects, make your products easy-to-use, and deliver top-notch documentation, a customer of yours will ultimately need help from you. Customers may consider the quality of your organization before they purchase a product from you. The responsiveness of your service and support organization, the support staff's knowledge and understanding of your product line, and their ability to resolve customer problems rapidly are all measures of the quality of your organization.

#### *Internal processes*

The quality of an organization is often judged by the processes followed by that organization. Your customers may ask the question, "Are you registered to ISO 9000?" and often base their purchase decision on the basis of whether your processes can be described in terms of a standard they trust. You should ask yourself this question: "If my customers were made aware of my processes, what opinion would they hold of my organization?"

## Quality Metrics

The quality attributes set represents your customers' quality requirements. Once defined, this information is used to help you answer two important product development questions: During the development process, *will* you produce a product that meets or exceeds these requirements? At the end of the development process, *have* you produced a product that meets or exceeds them? The first question must be asked repeatedly throughout the development process. When the answer to the question is negative, adjustments must be made to the process to bring the project back on course. Positive answers reassure that you are heading toward your goal to produce a product that meets or exceeds your customers' quality requirements. The second question is asked at the end as a final check, to make sure that a product was produced that will satisfy them. If the first question is asked often enough and solicits answers that provide conclusive evidence that you are heading toward your goal, the question asked at the end should readily confirm that an acceptable product has been produced.

Literally asking the question, "Are we building or have we built something that will ultimately meet or exceed customer requirements?" throughout the development process or at its conclusion will not provide you with the conclusive evidence that you seek. Imagine for a moment that you are a physician in an emergency room and a patient is brought to you for treatment. You ask your patient, "How are you feeling?" He replies, "Terrible!" Could you offer a treatment at that point? Not likely. To accurately diagnose the condition, you would perform specific tests such as measure heart rate, blood pressure, temperature, and so on. You may perform a series of tests designed to help you accurately determine the cause of their condition. You would then compare the results to what are considered normal results. Anything that falls outside of this normal range will most likely point to the cause of the malady. Once you have determined what is ailing the patient, you would prescribe a course of treatment. Hopefully, assuming that you ran the right tests, received accurate results, and prescribed the proper course of treatment, the patient will recover. To ensure that the patient is getting better, you would monitor progress by repeatedly applying tests and comparing them to the desired results. If your patient's condition began to drift away from the desired results, you would alter the treatment until you could see a trend leading toward the desired results.

The role of the quality assurance engineer is not unlike that of the physician. For each element of the customer quality attributes set, you must select and possibly create specific measurements that can be applied repeatedly during the development process and then again at its conclusion. The results of such measurements can be used to determine progress toward and finally attainment of quality goals.

### Types of metrics

Customer Oriented Software Quality Assurance divides software quality metrics into two categories: process and product. The metrics that are developed or selected for the production and maintenance of a product are determined by your customers' requirements as embodied by the quality attributes set. By placing your customer requirements ahead of internal requirements, and by involving them from the beginning of the development process, through delivery, and during maintenance, you maximize your ability to produce a product that will satisfy the quality requirements. If you ignore them until you are finished with development or wait until after the product is released, you will likely produce something that falls short of satisfying their requirements.

### Beyond metrics

Metrics provide you with a means to determine whether a product satisfies some set of requirements. Can metrics be selected from some bucket of metrics, or designed to allow you to determine whether your product satisfies your customers' quality requirements as expressed by their quality attributes set? Not always. Other ways to determine whether a product satisfies some set of requirements is through usability studies, checklists, and the like.

## Test Methods, Types, and Tools

Customer Oriented Software Quality Assurance defines a process that first captures customer requirements, representing them as quality attributes, and then translates those requirements into metrics. Testing is the means by which you determine whether a product meets or exceeds the baseline of acceptability established by the metrics. Using the patient-physician analogy, tests are the thermometers and sphygmomanometers of the quality assurance and test engineer.

Tests can be classified by method and type. You are probably already familiar with such terms as stress tests, system tests, unit tests, whitebox testing, blackbox testing, and so forth. Whitebox and blackbox testing are examples of test methods and stress tests, system tests, and unit tests are examples of test types. Selecting the right methods, the right test types, and then the right tests is perhaps the most challenging aspect of the Customer Oriented Software Quality Assurance methodology. Quite often, they are chosen arbitrarily. For example, stress tests, often designed to push a system beyond its design limits for some period of time, are frequently used to determine whether a product is ready for release. What if the product is never used in an environment that pushes it beyond its design limits? Is it necessary that such tests be used to determine if the product is ready for release? No. They might be used for other purposes, but not to determine whether the product is ready for release.

Once an appropriate method(s) and type(s) has been chosen, tests must be developed. Many choices exist here as well. For example, you may be able to purchase a commercial test suite to test your product. If you are developing a C compiler, there are several well-known C compiler test suites on the market. You may need to develop your own tests from scratch. You may also be able to purchase a test tool that simplifies the test development process.

### Test methods

A test method is simply a procedure one follows to create a set of tests that can be used to determine whether a product satisfies some set of quality related criteria. For Customer Oriented Software Quality Assurance, the quality related criteria includes meeting or exceeding customer quality requirements as defined by their quality attributes set. Therefore, the test methods chosen must support the attainment of that end.

The two most popular test methods are: blackbox and whitebox. The blackbox method ignores the details of what is inside the box. Whitebox tests are designed to exploit weaknesses in a product's design and implementation. For example, suppose that on examination of a product's design specification, a test engineer discovers that the application caches data in an in-memory cache until the user saves the file. A whitebox test could be developed that modifies a file then intentionally causes the system to reboot before a save operation is performed. In contrast, since the blackbox test method is applied without an awareness of the product's design and implementation, the test developer will likely fail to develop such test cases.

I have read about and participated in many debates concerning the use of these two methods. Many believe that only one test method or the other should be applied. My position is that the method or methods chosen should provide a means to an end. Achieving that end may require the application of more than one method. In those cases, combining methods becomes necessary. Strict conformance to one method or another will limit one's ability to achieve the desired end.

### Types of tests

Test cases are typically classified as one of the following types: unit, component, integration, system, scenario, or stress. Unit tests represent the least complex of the tests. Problems discovered by unit tests are typically the easiest problems to correct. Component tests tend to be more complex than unit tests and problems discovered by them are usually more difficult to correct. Each subsequent classification corresponds to an increasingly complicated set of test cases that tends to find problems that require lengthier analysis and defect fix times.

### Commercial test tools

As product complexity increases, development and QA cycles shorten, and companies continue to release products at an ever increasing rate, dependence on tools that simplify and improve the productivity of the quality assurance effort increases.

In addition to simplifying test development, test tools are available that gather certain metrics such as test coverage, number of lines of code, number of modules, number of function points, number of decision points, percentage of code executed by test cases, and so on. These tools are useful to the extent they allow you to determine whether your product satisfies your customers' quality attributes. For example, some companies define a code coverage metric that specifies the percentage of code that must be executed by test cases during the formal test phase of the product development cycle. What percentage of code must be covered to have a quality product? 90%? 100%? For practitioners of Customer Oriented Software Quality Assurance, the answers to such questions are found in the customer quality attributes set.

# Index